THE
NATIONAL
GALLERY

THE CHILDREN'S INTERACTIVE STORY OF ART

Susie Hodge

CARLTON
KiDS

THIS IS A CARLTON BOOK

Published in association with
National Gallery Company Limited

Text, design and illustration
© Carlton Books Limited 2015

Published in 2015 by
Carlton Books Limited,
An imprint of the
Carlton Publishing Group,
20 Mortimer Street,
London W1T 3JW

A catalogue record for this book is
available from the British Library.

ISBN: 978-1-78312-130-4

Printed and bound in China

Consultant: Rebecca Lyons
Illustrator: Rebecca Ashdown
Editor: Anna Brett
Design Manager: Emily Clarke
Designer: Emma Wicks
Production: Charlotte Cade
Picture Manager: Steve Behan
Publisher: Russell McLean

Picture Acknowledgements
The publishers would like to thank the following sources for their
kind permission to reproduce the pictures in this book.

Key: T=top, L=left, R=right, C=centre, B=bottom.

6. The Art Archive/Tate Gallery London/Eileen Tweedy, 7l. NG3862 Van Gogh, Chair © The National Gallery, London. Bought, Courtauld Fund, 1924, 7r. Getty Images/Lionel Bonaventure/AFP, 8l & 8r. Shutterstock.com, 9t. Thinkstock.com, 9b. Mariano via Wikipedia, 10. Getty Images/De Agostini, 11t. Bridgeman Images/British Museum, London, UK, 11b. Thinkstock.com, 12l. Getty Images/ Roger Viollet Collection, 12r., 13l., 13r., 14c, 14b, 15t. Shutterstock.com, 15b. Getty Images/Godong/Universal Images Group, 16t. Bridgeman Images/Photo © Boltin Picture Library, 16b. Topfoto/British Library Board, 17. Werner Forman Archive, 18t. Corbis/Marc Garanger, 18b. NG5115 Andrea di Bonaiuto da Firenze: The Virgin and Child with Ten Saints © The National Gallery, London. Presented by Mrs Richard F.P. Blennerhassett, 1940, 19t. NG1140 Duccio: The Healing of the Man Born Blind © The National Gallery, London, 19b. NG4451 The Wilton Diptych © The National Gallery, London, 20. Private Collection, 21t. NG5360 Giotto: Pentecost © The National Gallery, London. Bequeathed by Geraldine Emily Coningham in memory of her husband, Major Henry Coningham, and of Mrs Coningham of Brighton, 1942, 21b. Private Collection, 22t. NG3937 Domenico Ghirlandaio: The Virgin and Child © The National Gallery, London. Mond Bequest, 1924, 22b. NG665 Piero della Francesca: The Baptism of Christ © The National Gallery, London, 23t. NG915 Sandro Botticelli: Venus and Mars © The National Gallery, London, 23c. Private Collection, 23b. Shutterstock.com, 24. NG6275.1 Hans Memling: The Donne Triptych © The National Gallery, London. Acquired under the terms of the Finance Act from the Duke of Devonshire's Collection, 1957, 25tl. 25tl. NG653.2 Robert Campin: A Woman © The National Gallery, London, 25tr. NG653.1 Robert Campin: A Man © The National Gallery, London, 25b. NG4744 Hieronymus Bosch: Christ Mocked © The National Gallery, London, 26. NG186 Jan van Eyck: The Arnolfini Portrait, 1434 © The National Gallery, London, 27t. NG222 Jan van Eyck: Portrait of a Man, 1433 © The National Gallery, London, 27b. Bridgeman Images/Photo: Hugo Maertens, 28. NG6294 Paolo Uccello: Saint George and the Dragon © The National Gallery, London. Bought with a special grant and other contributions, 1959, 29tl. Shutterstock.com, 29tr. NG583 Paolo Uccello: The Battle of San Romano © The National Gallery, London, 29c. Getty Images/Johanna Leguerre/ AFP, 30. NG4255 Correggio: Christ taking leave of His Mother © The National Gallery, London. Presented by Lord Duveen, 1927, 31tl. Shutterstock.com, 31tr. NG1093 Leonardo da Vinci: The Virgin with the Infant Saint John the Baptist adoring the Christ Child accompanied by an Angel ('The Virgin of the Rocks') © The National Gallery, London, 31b. NG2919 Raphael: Procession to Calvary © The National Gallery, London, 32. NG809 Michelangelo: The Manchester Madonna © The National Gallery, London, 33t. Getty Images, 33b. Shutterstock.com, 34. NG35 Titian: Bacchus and Ariadne © The National Gallery, London, 35t. NG1326 Veronese: Allegory of Love: Happy Union © The National Gallery, London, 35b. NG16 Tintoretto: Saint George and the Dragon © The National Gallery, London. Holwell Carr Bequest, 1831, 36. NG6563 Albrecht Dürer, Saint Jerome © The National Gallery, London. Bought with the assistance of the Heritage Lottery Fund, The Art Fund and Mr J. Paul Getty Jr through the American Friends of the National Gallery, London, 1996, 37t. NG1314 Hans Holbein the Younger: The Ambassadors © The National Gallery, London, 37b. NG2211 Jan Gossaert: A Young Princess (Dorothea of Denmark?) © The National Gallery, London, 38t. NG651 Bronzino: Allegory with Venus and Cupid © The National Gallery, London, 38b. NG625 Brescia: The Madonna and Child with Saints © The National Gallery, London, 39tl. NG1131 Pontormo: Joseph with Jacob in Egypt © The National Gallery, London, 39tr. Bridgeman Images, 39b. Getty Images/DEA/P.Manusardi/Veneranda Biblioteca Ambrosiana, 41tl. NG6504 Caravaggio: Boy Bitten by a Lizard © The National Gallery, London. Bought with the aid of a contribution from the J. Paul Getty Jr Endowment Fund, 1986, 41tr. AKG-Images/MPortfolio/Electa, 41bl. NG6597 Annibale Carracci: The Holy Family with the Infant Saint John the Baptist © The National Gallery, London. Bought with the support of a number of gifts in wills and recent donations, 2004, 41br. NG1129 Diego Velazquez: Philip IV of Spain in Brown and Sliver © The National Gallery, London, 42. NG2568 Vermeer: Young Woman Seated at a Virginal © The National Gallery, London. Salting Bequest, 1910, 43t. NG6613 Ambrosius Bosschaert the Elder, A Still Life of Flowers in a Wan-Li Vase © The National Gallery, London. Accepted by HM Government in lieu of Inheritance Tax and allocated to the National Gallery,

2010, 43c. NG988 Jacob van Ruisdael, A Road winding between Trees towards a Distant Cottage © The National Gallery, London. Wynn Ellis Bequest, 1876, 43b. NG1256 Harmen Steenwyck: Still Life: An Allegory of the Vanities of Human Life © The National Gallery, London. Presented by Lord Savile, 1888, 44. NG6350 Rembrandt: Belshazzar's Feast © The National Gallery, London. Bought with a contribution from the Art Fund, 1964, 45tl. NG221 Rembrandt: Self-Portrait at the Age of 63 © The National Gallery, London, 45tc. NG672 Rembrandt: Self-Portrait at the Age of 34 © The National Gallery, London, 45r. NG1400 Rembrandt: Ecce Homo © The National Gallery, London, 46. NG278 Rubens: A Roman Triumph © The National Gallery, London, 47t. NG1172 Van Dyck: Equestrian Portrait of Charles I © The National Gallery, London, 47c. NG6518 Van Dyck: Lord John Stuart and his Brother, Lord Bernard Stuart © The National Gallery, London, 48c. NG6502 Van Dyck: The Balbi Children © The National Gallery, London, 48c. NG6519 Poussin: The Finding of Moses © The National Gallery, London. Bought jointly by the National Gallery and Amgueddfa Cymru – National Museum Wales with contributions from: J. Paul Getty Jnr (through the American Friends of the National Gallery, London), the National Heritage Memorial Fund, The Art Fund, Mrs Schreiber, the Esmée Fairbairn Foundation, the Moorgate Trusts, Sir Denis Mahon and anonymous donors, 1988, 48b. NG30 Claude: Seaport with the Embarkation of Saint Ursula © The National Gallery, London, 49t. Bridgeman Images/Bibliotheque Nationale, Paris, France, 49b. NG1449 Philippe de Champaigne: Cardinal de Richelieu © The National Gallery, London. Presented by Charles Butler, 1895, 50. NG2897 Jean-Antoine Watteau, The Scale of Love © The National Gallery, London, 51t. NG6445 Jean-Honoré Fragonard, Psyche showing her Sisters her Gifts from Cupid © The National Gallery, London, 51c. NG113 William Hogarth: Marriage A-la-Mode: The Marriage Settlement © The National Gallery, London, 51b. NG6440 François-Hubert Drouais, Madame de Pompadour at her Tambour Frame © The National Gallery, London, 52t. NG1101 Pietro Longhi, Exhibition of a Rhinoceros at Venice © The National Gallery, London, 52b. NG163 Canaletto, Venice: The Grand Canal with San Simeone Piccolo © The National Gallery, London. Bequeathed by Lord Farnborough, 1838, 53t. NG210 Francesco Guardi, Venice: Piazza San Marco, after 1780 © The National Gallery, London. Bequeathed by Richard Simmons, 1846, 53b. NG251 Giovanni Battista Tiepolo, The Virgin and Child appearing to a Group of Saints © The National Gallery, London. Salting Bequest, 1910, 54l. NG6569 George Stubbs, Whistlejacket, © The National Gallery, London. Bought with the support of the Heritage Lottery Fund, 1997, 54r. NG6495 Jacques-Louis David, Portrait of Jacobus Blauw © The National Gallery, London, 55l. NG725 Joseph Wright of Derby: An Experiment on a Bird in an Air Pump © The National Gallery, London. Presented by Edward Tyrrell, 1863, 55r. Getty Images/Marco Secchi, 56t. NG1473 Francisco de Goya, Doña Isabel de Porcel © The National Gallery, London, 56b. NG1909 Delaroche, Lady Jane Grey © The National Gallery, London. Bequeathed by the Second Lord Cheylesmore, 1902, 57t. NG6262 Eugene Delacroix, Ovid among the Scythians © The National Gallery, London, 57c. NG2423 Caspar David Friedrich, Winter Landscape © The National Gallery, London, 57b. NG1207 John Constable, The Hay Wain © The National Gallery, London. Presented by Henry Vaughan, 1886, 58. NG472 Joseph Mallord William Turner, Calais Pier © The National Gallery, London. Turner Bequest, 1856, 59t. NG524 Joseph Mallord William Turner, The Fighting Temeraire © The National Gallery, London. Turner Bequest, 1856, 59b. NG538 Joseph Mallord William Turner, Rain, Steam and Speed © The National Gallery, London. Turner Bequest, 1856, 60l. NG6447 Jean-François Millet, The Winnower © The National Gallery, London, 60r. NG3244 Honoré-Victorin Daumier, Don Quixote and Sancho Panza © The National Gallery, London. Sir Hugh Lane Bequest, 1917, 61t. NG621 Rosa Bonheur and Nathalie Micas, The Horse Fair © The National Gallery, London. Bequeathed by Jacob Bell, 1859, 61b. NG6596 Gustave Courbet, Beach Scene © The National Gallery, London. Bequeathed by Sir Robert Hart, Bt, 1971, 62. NG3858 Edouard Manet, Corner of a Café-Concert © The National Gallery, London. Bought, Courtauld Fund, 1924, 63t. Shutterstock.com, 63bl. NG6295 Hilaire-Germain-Edgar Degas, After the Bath, Woman drying herself © The National Gallery, London, 63br. NG4121 Hilaire-Germain-Edgar Degas, Miss La La at the Cirque Fernando © The National Gallery, London. Bought, Courtauld Fund, 1925, 64l. NG3268 Pierre-Auguste Renoir, The Umbrellas © The National Gallery, London. Sir Hugh Lane Bequest, 1917, 64b. NG4119 Camille Pissarro, The Boulevard Montmartre at Night © The National Gallery, London. Bought, Courtauld Fund, 1925, 65tl. Shutterstock.com, 65tc. NG6469 Hilaire-Germain-Edgar Degas, Hélène Rouart in her Father's Study © The National Gallery, London., 65r. NG3859 Pierre-Auguste Renoir, At the Theatre © The National Gallery, London. Bought, Courtauld Fund, 1923, 65b. NG3264 Berthe Morisot, Summer's

Day © The National Gallery, London. Sir Hugh Lane Bequest, 1917, 66. NG3951 Claude Monet, The Beach at Trouville © The National Gallery, London, 67t. NG6456 Claude Monet, Bathers at La Grenouillère © The National Gallery, London. Bequeathed by Mrs M.S. Walzer as part of the Richard and Sophie Walzer Bequest, 1979, 67c. NG6399 Claude Monet, The Thames Below Westminster, © The National Gallery, London. Bequeathed by Lord Astor of Hever, 1971, 67b. NG4240 Claude Monet, The Water Lily Pond, © The National Gallery, London, 68t. NG6421 Henri Rousseau, Surprised! © The National Gallery, London. Bought, with the aid of a substantial donation from the Hon. Walter H. Annenberg, 1972, 68b. NG4136 Paul Cézanne, Hillside in Provence © The National Gallery, London. Bought, Courtauld Fund, 1926, 69t. NG6609 Paul Gauguin, Bowl of Fruit and Tankard before a Window © The National Gallery, London. Bequeathed by Simon Sainsbury, 2006, 69b. NG3908 Seurat, Bathers at Asnières © The National Gallery, London. Bought, Courtauld Fund, 1924, 70c. NG3863 Vincent van Gogh, Sunflowers © The National Gallery, London. Bought, Courtauld Fund, 1924, 70bl. Library of Congress, Washington, 71t. NG3861 Vincent van Gogh, A Wheatfield, with Cypresses © The National Gallery, London. Bought, Courtauld Fund, 1923, 71b. NG3862 Van Gogh, Chair © The National Gallery, London. Bought, Courtauld Fund, 1924, 72l. NG6436 Gustave Moreau, Saint George and the Dragon © The National Gallery, London, 72r. NG6574 Akseli Gallen-Kallela, Lake Keitele © The National Gallery, London, 73t. NG6388 Vuillard: La Terrasse at Vasouy, The Garden © The National Gallery, London, 73b. NG6438 Redon, Ophelia among the Flowers © The National Gallery, London. Bought with a contribution from The Art Fund, 1977, 74. Bridgeman Images/Houses at L'Estaque, 1908 (oil on canvas), Braque, Georges (1882-1963)/Rupf Foundation, Bern, Switzerland. © ADAGP, Paris and DACS, London 2015, 75. Bridgeman Images/Mattioli Collection, Milan, Italy, 76. Bridgeman Images/Les Demoiselles d'Avignon, 1907 (oil on canvas), Picasso, Pablo (1881-1973)/Museum of Modern Art, New York, USA.© Succession Picasso/DACS, London 2015, 77. Bridgeman Images/Guernica, 1937 (oil on canvas), Picasso, Pablo (1881-1973)/Museo Nacional Centro de Arte Reina Sofia, Madrid, Spain.© Succession Picasso/DACS, London 2015, 78. NG6450 Matisse: Portrait of Greta Moll. Photo: © The National Gallery, London. Artwork: © Succession H. Matisse/ DACS 2015, 79t. Bridgeman Images/The Scream, 1893 (oil, tempera & pastel on cardboard), Munch, Edvard (1863-1944)/ Nasjonalgalleriet, Oslo, Norway, 79b. Bridgeman Images/Fate of the Animals, 1913, Marc, Franz (1880-1916)/Öffentliche Kunstsammlung, Basel, Switzerland, 80. Bridgeman Images/Fountain, 1917/64 (ceramic), Duchamp, Marcel (1887-1968)/The Israel Museum, Jerusalem, Israel/Vera & Arturo Schwarz Collection of Dada and Surrealist Art. © Succession Marcel Duchamp/ADAGP, Paris and DACS, London 2015, 81c. Bridgeman Images/ © Salvador Dali, Fundació Gala-Salvador Dalí, DACS, 2015, 81b. Bridgeman Images/Time Transfixed, 1938 (oil on canvas). © ADAGP, Paris and DACS, London 2015, 82. Bridgeman Images/ Suprematist Composition, 1915 (oil on canvas), Malevich, Kazimir Severinovich (1878-1935)/Stedelijk Museum, Amsterdam, The Netherlands, 83. Bridgeman Images/Composition with Red, Blue and Yellow, 1930, Oil on canvas, 46 x 46 cm, Kunsthaus Zurich, 84. Bridgeman Images/American Gothic, 1930 (oil on board), Wood, Grant (1891-1942)/The Art Institute of Chicago, IL, USA, 85. Red, Orange, Orange on Red, 1962 (oil on canvas), Rothko, Mark (1903-70)/Saint Louis Art Museum, Missouri, USA/Funds given by the Shoenberg Foundation, Inc. © Georgia O'Keeffe Museum/DACS, 2015, 86. Bridgeman Images/Lavender Mist: Number 1, 1950 (oil, enamel & aluminium paint on canvas), Pollock, Jackson (1912-56) / National Gallery of Art, Washington DC, USA. © The Pollock-Krasner Foundation ARS, NY and DACS, London 2015, 87. Bridgeman Images/Red, Orange, Orange on Red, 1962 (oil on canvas), Rothko, Mark (1903-70) / Saint Louis Art Museum, Missouri, USA/Funds given by the Shoenberg Foundation, Inc. © 1998 Kate Rothko Prizel & Christopher Rothko ARS, NY and DACS, London, 88. Bridgeman Images/Campbell's Soup Can, 1962 (screen print), Warhol, Andy (1928-87) /Saatchi Collection, London, UK. © 2015 The Andy Warhol Foundation for the Visual Arts, Inc./Artists Rights Society (ARS), New York and DACS, London, 89t. Bridgeman Images/Supermarket Shopper, 1970 (polyester resin figure and various media), Hanson, Duane (1925-96)/Ludwig Collection, Aachen, Germany. © Estate of Duane Hanson/VAGA, New York/DACS, London 2015, 89b. Tate Images/© Estate of Roy Lichtenstein/DACS 2015, 90. Getty Images/Ed Jones/ AFP. © Tracey Emin. All rights reserved, DACS 2015, 91. Shutterstock.com/© Estate of Robert Smithson/DACS, London/VAGA, New York 2015, 92. © The National Gallery, London, 93t & c & cr © The National Gallery, London.

Every effort has been made to acknowledge correctly and contact the source and/ or copyright holder of each picture and Carlton Books Limited apologizes for any unintentional errors or omissions, which will be corrected in future editions of this book.

Contents

The pages highlighted in a colour are our featured artists – find out about their life, style and work in detail here.

HOW TO USE YOUR FREE APP

HOW DOES IT WORK?

Your app uses Augmented Reality (AR) which mixes the real and the virtual worlds together, so that a mobile device with a camera can bring books to life with amazing interactive animations.

WHAT DO I NEED?

To run the Augmented Reality animations, all you need is this book and a device that meets the minimum system requirements (see below).

HOW TO USE AR

It's easy! Here's what you have to do...

1 Download the free ArtGalleryAR iOS app from the Apple App Store or the ArtGalleryAR Android app from Google Play.

2 Launch the ArtGalleryAR app to open the home page. Tap one of the buttons to begin.

3 Hold your mobile device up to pages 92–93 to start your art gallery experience. Allow the app to access your photos if you want to upload images of your own artwork.

WHAT YOUR APP CONTAINS

Your home screen allows you to access the virtual gallery and the games, as well as help and a link to buy the book.

Create your own virtual gallery by uploading images of paintings from The National Gallery into the frames.

Decide on a theme for each room in the gallery. Which paintings work best together? Upload your own images and hang them next to the masters if you want!

Try your luck at the three art activity games in the app. Can you piece together the jigsaw, spot the differences and pick the odd one out?

System Requirements
• Apple devices using iOS 6.0 minimum: iPhone 4S and above; iPad2 and above; iPhone Touch 5th Gen. and above
• Android devices with both front and back cameras using Android 4.0 and above. ARMv7 processors.

NEED SOME HELP?

If you've got a problem, check out our website:

www.carltonbooks.co.uk/art/help

What is art?

Lots of people have different ideas about art. Many believe that good art is realistic paintings or sculpture. Some say it is awe-inspiring buildings. Many think that art should be beautiful, or skilful, or be something that makes us think, or that it should inspire and uplift us.

OPINIONS

And guess what? All the opinions above are right, because there is no one, agreed-upon definition of art. Art can be many things, from lifelike to abstract, or pretty to ugly. It can be ornaments or architecture, drawing or **installations**. It can make you laugh, cry or feel cross. It can be large or small, colourful or plain, conventional or rebellious ... and a lot more.

✪ Did you know?

There are stories throughout the history of art that tell of artists and critics getting angry with each other over their differences of opinions about art. When the great artist J.M.W. Turner (1775–1851) exhibited a painting of a snow storm at sea, a critic complained that the painting looked like a mass of soapsuds and whitewash. Turner was furious! "Soapsuds and whitewash!" he was heard to mutter. "What would they have? I wonder what they think the sea's like? I wish they'd been in it."

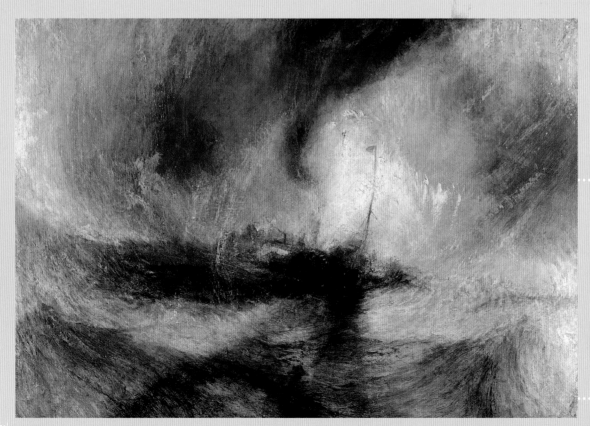

Snow-Storm, Steamboat off a Harbour's Mouth, J.M.W. Turner, 1842, oil on canvas, Tate, London, UK. Turner's snow storm captures **atmosphere**, not details.

Artists often make different marks to create a variety of effects. With a pencil and ruler, draw a grid on a sheet of paper. Using a sharp 2B pencil, in each space make different marks such as dots, lines, squiggles or zig-zags.

Cave paintings in southwestern France, estimated to be about 20,000 years old. This is some of the oldest art we know about.

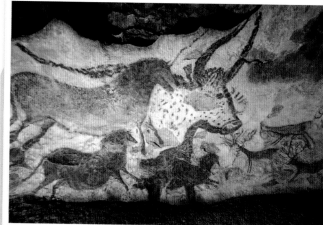

Chair, Vincent van Gogh, 1888, oil on canvas, National Gallery, London, UK. Thick paint showing an old chair went against accepted styles of art.

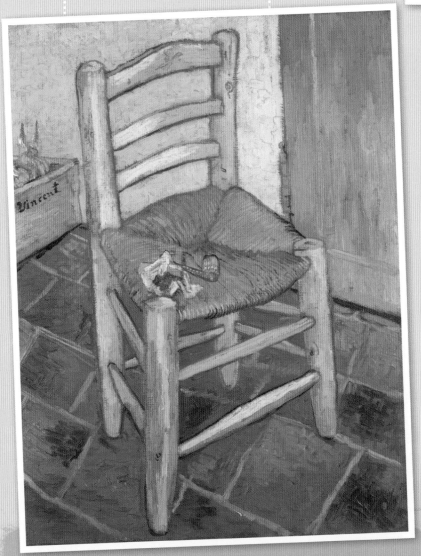

FROM CAVES TO TOILETS

We know that humans have made art for thousands of years, for different reasons and with different results. Even before inventing writing, people were creating art. Artists often try out new things and their work is sometimes seen as shocking.

For instance, in 1917, Marcel Duchamp (1887–1968) bought a urinal and displayed it in an exhibition, calling it *Fountain*. He had not made it, and did not pretend that he had. He exhibited it upside-down, and signed a name on it – not his – in black paint. People were horrified! But Duchamp was trying to make a point that everyday objects can be art if the artist says they are or depending on where and how they are displayed. He was questioning the role of the artist and what we call art.

✪ Did you know?

Some of the most famous works of art ever made include: a picture of a banker's wife, a protest about war, an old chair, a dream, and a messy, unmade bed.

From axes to art

OUR PREHISTORIC ANCESTORS

Prehistoric art means art that was made by people before they had invented writing. The invention and development of writing happened at different times and in different places all over the world. As some cultures invented their own forms of writing, the art they made (and wrote about) was no longer classed as prehistoric.

THE EARLIEST ART

There have been humans on Earth for over four million years, but the first evidence we have of humans deliberately making carved or painted objects was around 35,000 years ago. Some of the earliest art ever found includes little, plump, carved stone female figures from Germany. Dating from just a bit later are hundreds of paintings in caves, discovered in countries including France, Spain and Indonesia. These are often pictures of animals such as lions, horses and bison. Other ancient art has been found where artists carved or cut into rocks. For instance, in Utah, USA in about 150 CE, Native American artists scratched pictures into rocks, revealing lighter sandstone beneath. These rock engravings are called petroglyphs.

Petroglyphs, c.150 CE, Newspaper Rock, Utah, USA. About 2,000 years old, these petroglyphs were made by cutting, scraping and carving on to rock surfaces.

WHAT DOES IT MEAN?

We know little about these early artists, why the art was made or what it meant. Cave art was made deep inside caves, where there was no light and artists painted by the dim glow of flickering fires. Much of it was probably believed to have magic powers or was made to ask the spirits for success in hunting.

CLUES ABOUT THE PAST

On some cave walls in Libya, Africa, are pictures of giraffes and other grazing animals – but the caves are in deserts where there are no plants for the animals to eat! The pictures were painted in about 12,000 BCE, which suggests that the desert was once a lush landscape where animals ate plants and grass.

✪ Did you know?

Artists made their colours from crushed earth, rocks, plant stems and leaves, and mixed them with animal fat or water. They applied this with their fingers, bones or brushes made from plants. In some places like Altamira in Spain, wooden scaffolding is believed to have been made so that the artists could paint high on the cave roofs.

Stencilled hand prints made by prehistoric people, c.11,000–7,500 BCE, Río Pinturas, Argentina.

HAND PRINTS

Some of the oldest images that have been found are hand **prints** on cave walls made by families. Adults and children placed their hands against walls and blew pigment over them through hollow sticks or bones. When they took their hands away, their hand shapes were left on the walls.

Myths, mysteries and monuments

THE ART OF ANCIENT EGYPT

Beginning in about 3100 BCE, the ancient Egyptian civilization lasted for about 3,000 years. During that time, a vast amount of art was produced, from colourful paintings to impressive sculpture and buildings. The art was mainly concerned with religious beliefs, but some art relates to daily life.

HIEROGLYPHS

The word hieroglyph means 'sacred carving'. Hieroglyphics are simple pictures or diagrams, and one of the first forms of writing, invented by the Egyptians early in their existence. There are about 750 different hieroglyphs. Most are pictures of people, animals and plants, and it took students about twelve years to learn to write using them!

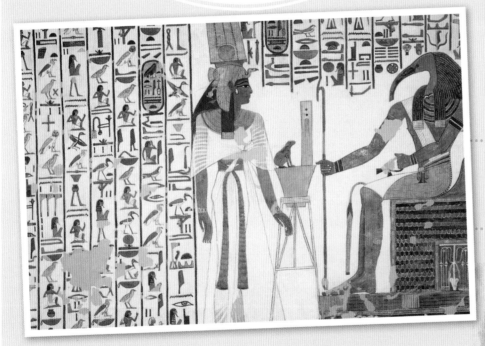

Painting on papyrus of Nefertari, the favourite wife of the Pharaoh Ramesses II, in front of the god Thoth, with hieroglyphs.

GODS AND THE AFTERLIFE

Firmly believing in their gods and the afterlife, ancient Egyptians created art for religious buildings and tombs. Pictures and artefacts showed the gods how dead people had lived, and tombs were filled with things that the dead might need in the afterlife, such as furniture, games and weapons. As tombs were either buried in the sand or inside huge, closed pyramids, many survived, giving us detailed images of the ancient Egyptian civilization and their artistic treasures.

✪ Did you know?

The Great Pyramid of Giza was built around 2575–2465 BCE and has over two million stone blocks, precisely cut, each weighing at least 2.5 tonnes. It was originally covered with highly polished limestone that shimmered in the sun.

Make a flat Egyptian-style picture that tells someone else about you and your life. Draw people's heads, feet and arms from the side, but eyes from the front. If you include animals, make them quite realistic.

Fowling in the Marshes, c.1350 BCE, British Museum, London, UK. A wall painting of a man called Nebamun hunting.

ART RULES

Ancient Egyptian art usually followed strict rules. Everything was measured and put in place for a purpose. All art, including statues, paintings, reliefs and buildings, was mathematically arranged, created with grids, and every artist had to learn the rules of representation. This meant that, for example, statues of seated people had their hands on their knees, eyes in pictures were shown from the front, but heads and arms from the side. Men were larger and darker skinned than women.

SCENES OF EVERYDAY LIFE

As wall paintings were made to help the dead in the afterlife, they showed everyday activities. Pictures were full of symbols, which the ancient Egyptians understood.

Book of the Dead. A scroll of papyrus, featuring spells for a dead person's journey to the afterlife. It was placed in the burial chamber.

BOOK OF THE DEAD

A wealthy or important person was usually buried with his or her Book of the Dead, which was a papyrus scroll containing spells and pictures – called vignettes – that helped that person reach the afterlife, and illustrated what would happen on arrival.

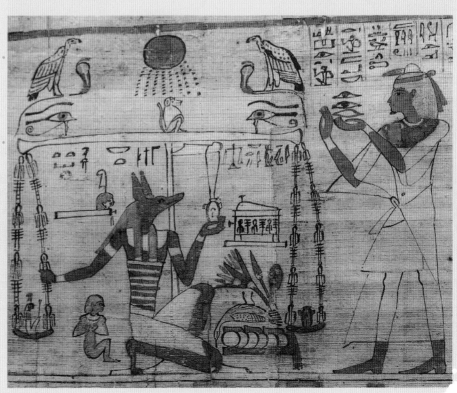

The great creators

ANCIENT GREECE AND ROME

For over 1,000 years, the ancient Greeks and Romans produced sculpture, paintings and architecture. The Greeks aimed for perfection and the Romans aimed for **realism**.

GREEK COLUMNS

Columns were used all over ancient Greece to hold up buildings, rooftops and temples. They were made in three styles: Doric, Ionic and Corinthian.

Doric columns (left) are the simplest, Ionic columns (centre) have scroll shapes, and Corinthian columns (right) are the fanciest.

PERFECT PROPORTIONS

Ancient Greek artists worked out proportions to achieve the appearance of perfection. They often portrayed gods, who they thought were like extra-beautiful, grand people. The earliest Greek statues were rigid-looking, but by about the 6th century BCE, sculptors began to study the human body, and they often sculpted athletes who had perfect bodies and wore no clothes when they practised sports.

Discobolus, Myron of Eleutherae, c.450 BCE, marble, Vatican Museum, Vatican City. This is a Roman copy of an ancient Greek bronze statue. An athlete is twisting to throw his discus.

GREEK PAINTING AND SCULPTURE

Painting was one of the most important types of art in ancient Greece, but few paintings have survived as they were made on walls that have since been destroyed. Many ancient Greek marble statues and temples were painted in bright colours, and many bronze statues were made with the lost wax process, when wax was moulded around a clay model, then more clay shaped around the wax. The wax was melted and molten bronze poured in. When the bronze set, the clay was removed. Statues stood in temples and town streets.

Red-figure vase. With red figures on black, the style developed in ancient Greece after black-figure painting.

Mosaic from the Villa Romana del Casale, Sicily, Italy. An ancient Roman mosaic of female athletes.

POTTERY

Greek and Roman pots were so widely produced that thousands of pieces have survived. The Greeks had two main methods of decorating pottery: black-figure and red-figure style. Both were made with red clay, but the areas that remain red were painted before the pottery was heated in a kiln.

⭐ Did you know?

The Pantheon was a Roman temple built for the gods in 117–125 CE. At the time, the roof – 43 metres (142 feet) in diameter – was the largest dome ever built. It was so huge that to hold it up, the brick and concrete walls were six metres (20 feet) thick! A hole in the top of the dome – the oculus – is open to the sky.

THE POWER OF ROME

By 100 CE, Rome ruled over most of the then-known world. Romans employed artists and workmen throughout their empire to create art and architecture. Like the Greeks, Roman art and architecture was used to honour the gods, but also to celebrate events or to show their power, and they liked realistic art.

Looking eastwards

ISLAMIC ART

From the 7th century, when Europe was going through what is often called the 'Dark Ages', the Islamic world was starting a golden age of learning. The Islamic faith spread rapidly across the Middle East and into Asia and Africa. Huge advances were made in art, architecture, mathematics, science, medicine and astronomy.

★

BLENDING STYLES

At first, Islamic art was influenced by the different countries and traditions that had become part of Arab world. So the art was often a blend of Arab, Turkish, Persian, Indian, Roman and Byzantine styles.

Carpet weaving began in Persia (Iran) over 2,500 years ago. Patterns were woven into wool, silk and cotton, and the carpets became known all over the world.

FINE CRAFTS

Islamic art describes a vast range of art that was produced in lands where the rulers were Muslim. Islamic art is not always religious, and crafts, such as pottery and textiles, are just as important as painting and sculpture. Fine crafts, including Persian carpets and richly ornamented **ceramics** and enamelled glass, have been hugely influential across the world.

GEOMETRIC PATTERNS

As many Islamic traditions forbid images of humans, geometric designs and patterns became common. The way some geometric patterns can be continuous is thought to help viewers think about life and the greatness of creation.

Made of jasper, onyx, marble and granite, these are some of the 856 patterned arches in the Great Mosque of Córdoba, Spain.

INDIVIDUAL STYLES

By about 1000 CE, the Islamic Empire was spreading, and art styles developed individually in countries such as in Spain, India, Egypt and Persia. In some places, rules against using images of people were relaxed. In Persia for instance, artists created miniature paintings of people at court, or famous people in history.

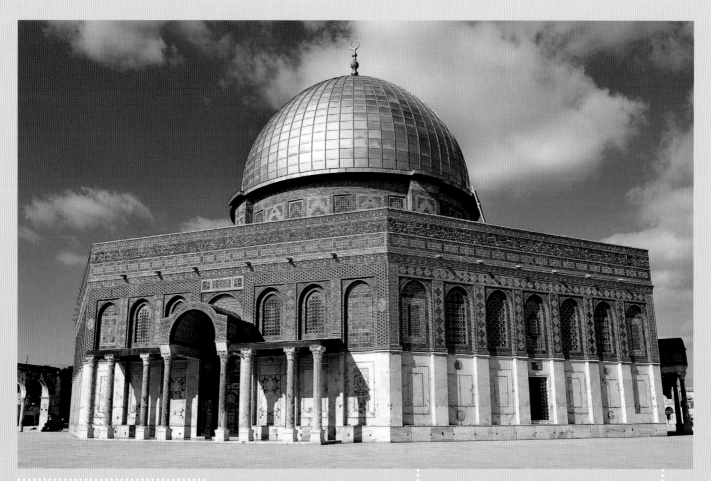

Initially completed in 691 CE, the Dome of the Rock, Jerusalem, is one of the oldest works of Islamic architecture.

MOSAICS

Mosques and other Islamic buildings were frequently decorated with intricate **mosaics** and carved or painted arabesques (ornate repeated patterns). Some of the earliest Islamic art can be seen in the elaborate Roman-style mosaics on the Dome of the Rock mosque in Jerusalem, the Great Mosque in Damascus, the Great Mosque in Córdoba and the Alhambra Palace in Granada.

⭐ Did you know?

Tesserae is the name of the tiny – usually cubed – pieces of stone, glass or marble used to make mosaics. Islamic artists carefully cut the marble, stone or coloured glass and then placed them in wet plaster, creating designs and patterns. Sometimes they backed glass tesserae with metal foil so the mosaics glittered.

CALLIGRAPHY

Calligraphy – or fancy writing – has always been important in Islamic culture. Calligraphy was often used to write the Qur'an or sacred inscriptions to decorate objects and buildings, and has been influential in many non-Islamic arts.

The golden age of China

The Tang Dynasty (618–906 CE) is often described as a golden age of achievement, when China prospered and trade and art flourished. Tang Dynasty art is often called the Classical period of Chinese art and literature, as it set high standards that later poets, painters and sculptors tried to match.

★

CAPTURING THE SPIRIT

Painters aimed to capture the spirit of their subjects rather than detailed, life-like images. Sculpture was also important, especially in Buddhist art, which emphasized the grace, power and kindness of the Buddha and his attendants.

This sculpture was created in the 8th century. It expresses Buddha's wisdom and serenity.

THE FINEST ARTISTS AND CRAFTSMEN

Tang emperors were particularly enthusiastic about art. Across China, they ordered new palaces, temples, pagodas and tombs – built and decorated with all kinds of art. They also encouraged artists to create sculpture, paintings, carvings, textiles, glass and metalwork. When Emperor Xuanzong ruled (626–49) from Chang'an, the largest city in the world at the time, he attracted some of the greatest artists in China.

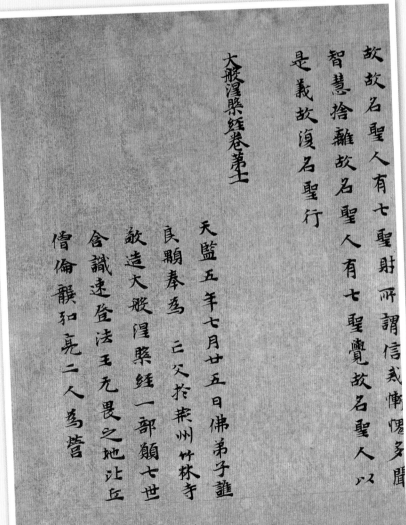

The Tang Dynasty produced the largest number of calligraphers in Chinese history.

FLOWING LINES

Through the empire's success in trade along the land and maritime Silk Roads, ideas between China and other countries were exchanged, and artists developed new ideas and skills. For the first time, painters did not paint just religious images, but also landscapes, known as 'shanshui' (mountain-water), and scenes from history and everyday life at court. Painters focused on nature, made people look realistic, and used flowing lines to portray movement. Delicate brush-and-ink pictures with washes of colour conveyed atmosphere and depth.

One of the best-known landscape artists was Wang Wei (699–759), while Zhou Fang (c.730–800) painted court ladies, and Han Gan (c.706–783) painted pictures of the Emperor's horses. The greatest Tang artist of figure painting was Wu Daozi (c.680–760), who applied vigorous brushstrokes, creating expressive, energetic pictures.

✪ Did you know?

Wu Daozi was so admired that legends around his artistry developed about him. He was supposed to have imitated with his brush the whirling movement of General Pei Min's famous sword dance. In one temple he painted five dragons so realistic that their scales would shimmer in flight, and whenever it was about to rain, a mist would rise from them.

Sowing the seeds

GOTHIC ART

During the 12th century, Europe's population grew and great churches and cathedrals were built, first in northern France and then across Europe. These huge, light and airy buildings had richly coloured stained glass windows, carved statues, pointed arches, and towers and spires that seemed to soar up to Heaven. People spent a lot of time at church, and the wealthy church members paid artists to paint and sculpt Christian stories on wooden panels, in window glass and in statues and carvings.

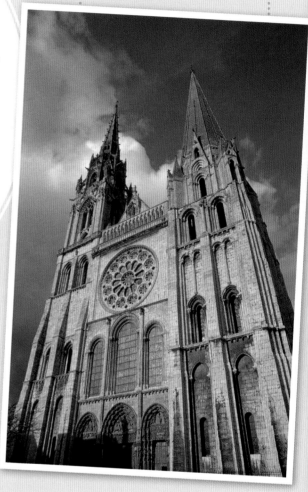

EXPRESSIVE FACES

Art was useful to remind people of religious stories, as most people could not read or write. Before the 12th century, medieval artists painted and sculpted in a set way – bodies looked stiff and faces were expressionless. Then, as the vast churches and cathedrals were built, the art became more intricate. The style later came to be called **Gothic**.

Artists tried to express Christian beliefs and to show stories from the Bible and saints' lives as they might have appeared in real life, so they created facial expressions, and garments that had folds and wrinkles. Painters also began using brighter colours than previously, more like the brilliant colours of manuscript illuminations (illustrations).

The Healing of the Man Born Blind, Duccio di Buoninsegna, 1307/8–11, egg tempera on wood, The National Gallery, London, UK. Duccio's work is more realistic and expressive than most other paintings of the time.

DUCCIO

In the early 14th century, Duccio di Buoninsegna (active 1278–died 1319) painted the *Maestà* for Siena Cathedral. It was one of the largest altarpieces ever produced, with lots of panels making up the whole work, all showing stories from the New Testament about the life of Jesus. It became hugely influential as Duccio shaded the faces and clothes so they appeared more **three-dimensional** than paintings had done before, and he gave the figures sweet, kind expressions. When Duccio completed it, the painting was so admired that the leaders of Siena gave everyone in the city a holiday so they could watch it being carried triumphantly to the cathedral!

PRIVATE PRAYER

Some altarpieces were made to be portable, so that people who owned them could say their prayers anywhere. *The Wilton Diptych* was one of these, made for King Richard II who ruled England from 1377 to 1399. It meant that wherever he was, the King could pray before it. A diptych is a painting, carving or piece of metalwork on two panels, usually hinged like a book. *The Wilton Diptych* shows Richard II with angels and saints, kneeling as he is presented to the Virgin and Child. No one knows who painted it, but it is important as it shows us how painting developed in northern Europe during the Gothic era.

The Wilton Diptych, artist unknown, c.1395–99, egg tempera on oak, The National Gallery, London, UK. This portable altarpiece made for King Richard II is painted in the Gothic style, using costly materials.

19

Giotto

While Duccio was painting in Siena, not far away in Florence was another painter who also became famous for changing art. Giotto di Bondone (1267–1337) painted in a way that seemed startlingly realistic to onlookers and helped them imagine Bible stories as if they were happening in front of them. Like Duccio, Giotto painted Bible figures with lifelike faces and clothes, but he also gave them expressions that showed different emotions, which was fairly unusual at the time.

PAINTING STORIES

As most of the population of Europe could not read at that time, being told Bible stories in church and looking at paintings and statues was for their education and entertainment as well as for their devotions. So Giotto deliberately made his paintings interesting – like comics without words. Many artists after him followed his ideas.

Madonna and the Child Enthroned with Saints, Giotto di Bondone, c.1310, tempera on panel, Uffizi Gallery, Florence, Italy. Giotto gave his figures lifelike expressions.

BECOMING PART OF THE WALL

As well as making large paintings to hang up in churches, Giotto also painted pictures directly on to church and chapel walls using the **fresco** painting technique. Fresco is the Italian word for fresh, and it describes a technique of painting on to freshly plastered walls. To make a fresco, a wall is coated with fine plaster, then pigments (powdered colour) are mixed with water and painted on to the plaster. When the paint dries, it becomes part of the wall. Giotto used both 'buon fresco' and 'fresco secco' techniques. Buon fresco means 'true' fresco and is when paint is applied to wet plaster, and fresco secco means 'dry' fresco, when paint is applied to plaster that has already dried. In fresco secco, egg yolk is added to pigment to make it stick.

MAKING IT REAL

Unlike any other medieval artist, Giotto tried to make his figures look solid. Dramatic gestures emphasized their emotions and brought Bible stories alive for viewers. The way he arranged his pictures, sometimes putting people behind others, created a powerful sense of space and made flat pictures seem to have depth. Famous during his lifetime, Giotto worked in several Italian cities, including Florence, Assisi, Padua and Naples.

Pentecost, Giotto di Bondone and workshop, 1310–18, egg tempera on poplar, The National Gallery, London, UK. Giotto was one of the first artists to overlap figures as they appear in real life.

✪ Did you know?

In Giotto's time, successful artists had busy workshops with lots of assistants to help them. Assistants usually spent years learning all the artists' skills. They learned to prepare pigments and panels, and they copied the master artist's style. When they had studied for some time, they were trusted to draw, paint or sculpt parts of the master's work.

The Arrest of Christ (The Kiss of Judas), Giotto di Bondone, c.1304–6, fresco, Scrovegni Chapel, Padua, Italy. An example of how Giotto draped his figures realistically and created human emotions on the faces.

A new type of beauty

THE EARLY RENAISSANCE IN ITALY

In the 15th and 16th centuries, artists and architects in Italy started rediscovering ancient Roman artefacts and began learning from their styles and skills. Some new ideas were also developing, suggesting that rather than concentrating so much on getting to heaven, people's achievements should also be celebrated during their lives. This was called humanism.

HUMANISM

Humanism was a way of thinking. One aspect was that people should strive to improve themselves and be educated in the arts, literature and science. Humanists also preferred art that looked at the real world, at nature and human behaviour, and many artists believed that by making art, they could explore the inner workings of the world. So art began to be created that explored more ideas than just religion.

The Virgin and Child, Domenico Ghirlandaio, c.1480–90, tempera on poplar, The National Gallery, London, UK. This delicate work was painted by Michelangelo's teacher.

REBIRTH

All the changes and developments in art, thinking, education and science, later became known as **the Renaissance**, which means rebirth. It was how people looking back saw the period – a rebirth of ancient culture, learning and art. The Renaissance began in Florence and then spread to other parts of Italy. Florence became rich with the wool trade and banking, and the wealthy people wanted to decorate their palaces. They looked for new styles, based on old or ancient art and so Greek and Roman ideas were reborn. Italy was made up of independent city-states, like mini-countries, at this time, and as these city-states tried to rival each other, ideas in art spread.

The Baptism of Christ, Piero della Francesca, 1450, egg tempera on poplar, The National Gallery, London, UK. In clear colours and accurate **linear perspective**, Jesus is being baptized.

Venus and Mars, Sandro Botticelli, c.1485, tempera and oil on panel, The National Gallery, London, UK. Botticelli often painted ancient Greek and Roman **myths**.

CREATIVE BUZZ

From the start of the Renaissance, there was a great buzz of creativity as artists began producing art with more lifelike skills. Donatello (1386–1466) made incredibly realistic statues, Masaccio (1401–28) a mathematician as well as an artist, created a sense of depth. Piero della Francesca (c.1415/20–92) also mixed art and maths, painting light, balanced pictures often in fresco. Sandro Botticelli (1445–1510) painted graceful curving lines and delicate faces. Giovanni Bellini (c.1430–1516) used rich colours and expressed subtle emotions. Domenico Ghirlandaio (1449–94) included well-observed details and Lorenzo Ghiberti (1378–1455) created detailed, **low relief** sculptures on some huge bronze doors in Florence that were so breathtaking they were nicknamed *The Gates of Paradise*.

Très Riches Heures, Limbourg Brothers, c.1412–16, parchment, Musée Condé, Chantilly, France. This was painted just before the Renaissance began.

The Gates of Paradise, Lorenzo Ghiberti, 1425–52, bronze, Florence Baptistery. These doors are replicas of the originals which are now in the Museo dell'Opera del Duomo.

THE POWERFUL MEDICI

One of the most powerful Italian families was the Medici, who lived in Florence. They became famous for spending a lot of money encouraging the arts and humanism. They and some other powerful Italian families, including the Sforza of Milan, the Este of Ferrara and the Gonzaga of Mantua, had a major influence on the Renaissance.

A new type of reality

THE RENAISSANCE IN NORTHERN EUROPE

In northern Europe, the Renaissance remained more influenced by Gothic art than ancient Rome. Although northern artists knew what was happening in Italy, they went in a different direction. They still aimed for realism, but instead of copying ancient statues, they represented real people and everyday situations. In the Netherlands, some time in the 15th century, painters also began using a new invention – **oil paint**.

OIL PAINT

Oil paint was easier to blend and could be used to create fine detail, and it dried slowly, which meant that painters could make changes and improvements as they worked. Northern artists loved it! To make oil paints, they mixed their pigments with plant oils, such as linseed or walnut. In Italy, most artists were still painting with quick-drying tempera, which was pigment mixed with egg yolk.

CLOSE DETAILS

While Italian artists were busy working out lines and angles of linear perspective (see page 28), in some parts of northern Europe, artists were painting and sculpting close details of the world, often using **symbolism** that viewers understood. For example, the wheel for Saint Catherine or the tower for Saint Barbara, as in *The Donne Triptych*. Their paintings also often showed religious scenes as if they were happening at that time in ordinary houses. The aim of these artists was to create images of a world that viewers could recognize. So, for instance, Saint Joseph the carpenter might be portrayed woodworking in a contemporary house, or Mary, the mother of Jesus, could be shown in a living room with her baby.

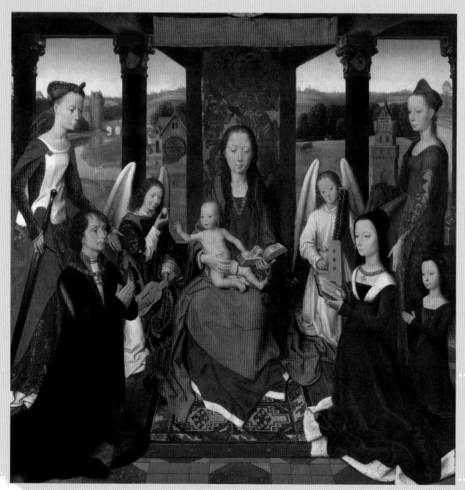

The Donne Triptych, Hans Memling, c.1478, oil on oak, The National Gallery, London, UK. Mary and the baby Jesus are surrounded by angels, as well as Sir John Donne and his wife and daughter, the **patrons** of the work.

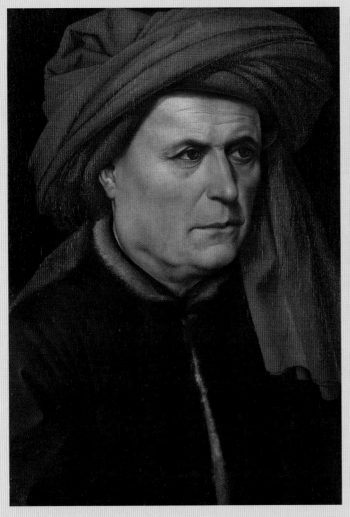

PICTURES OF HELL

Some painters in the north envisaged fantasy worlds showing people trapped in Hell and eaten by monsters. This was to remind people to behave well so that they could go to Heaven instead. The paintings of Hieronymus Bosch (1450–1516) were sometimes like nightmares or dream worlds, and he depicted ugly, cruel faces to show people behaving badly.

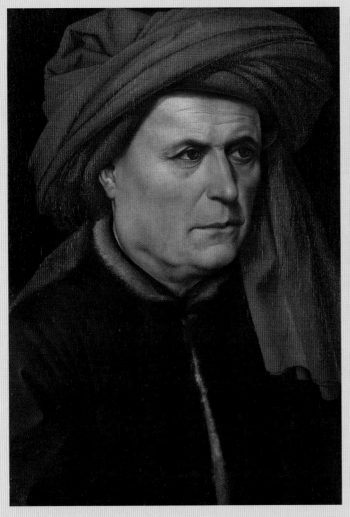

Christ Mocked (The Crowning with Thorns), Hieronymus Bosch, c.1490–1500, oil on oak, The National Gallery, London, UK.

THE MOST SKILFUL ARTISTS

As well as art that was made for churches and cathedrals, across the countries of northern Europe royalty, powerful nobles and wealthy private citizens **commissioned** art for their homes and private chapels. Some of the most skilful painters there included Jan van Eyck (1395–1441), Robert Campin (c.1378–1444), Roger van der Weyden (1400–64), Hugo van der Goes (1440–82), and Hans Memling (active 1465–died 1494). Although each artist adapted to their local customs and preferences, each one created extraordinarily realistic detail in their work.

Van Eyck

One of the first artists to use oil paint, Jan van Eyck painted clear, lifelike **portraits**, altarpieces and private scenes. Born in the Netherlands, he attracted many powerful patrons (people who bought his work), including the Duke of Burgundy, rich merchants and members of the Church.

THE ARNOLFINI PORTRAIT

In 1434, van Eyck painted this double portrait of a wealthy Italian merchant, Giovanni Arnolfini, and his wife. The detailed, lustrous painting seems to depict two people inside, but it is also full of hidden meanings. Van Eyck has created the illusion of the inside of a room, furnished with costly things – a carpet, velvet coverings and oranges (it was expensive to buy oranges in northern Europe at the time).

The Arnolfini Portrait, Jan van Eyck, 1434, oil on oak, The National Gallery, London, UK.

SYMBOLISM

The lady holds up her green dress but she is not pregnant, and the shape of her folded dress is simply fashionable. The dog is a symbol of faithfulness or fidelity – as dogs are known to be faithful animals. In the convex mirror on the wall is a reflection of the scene and another couple, one of whom may be van Eyck. Above the mirror, the artist signed his work: "Jan van Eyck was here". This is an unusual way to sign a work of art, and has led to all kinds of suggestions about why van Eyck signed it the way he did. It may be simply that he wanted to suggest how lifelike or real he felt his portrait of Arnolfini to be.

Although van Eyck uses lots of bright colours, he made them from just a few pigments. His **palette** included one white, two yellows, four reds, four greens, one blue and one black. By mixing these colours in different combinations, he made many more. He also used glazes, which are transparent layers of paint applied over other, dried layers of opaque (not see-through) paint.

Portrait of a Man, Jan van Eyck, 1433, oil on oak, The National Gallery, London, UK.

REALISTIC FACES

In *Portrait of a Man*, 1433, both soft, subtle and dramatic tonal contrasts or dark and light shading make the image look **3D**. Carefully drawn features and realistic-looking textures make a startlingly lifelike portrait. Look at the veins in the eyes and the stubble on the man's chin. Many people believe this is a self-portrait of van Eyck. In his huge masterpiece, the *Ghent Altarpiece* (1430–2), probably painted with his brother Hubert, he painted 330 heads – and made every face completely different and lifelike.

Ghent Altarpiece, probably Hubert and Jan van Eyck, 1432, oil and tempera on panel, Cathedral of Saint Bavo, Ghent, Belgium.

JEWEL COLOURS

Van Eyck used oil paints in thin layers called glazes, creating rich, jewel-bright colours that could not be achieved with tempera. With this method, he created the appearance of all sorts of textures, including shining metal, soft fur or velvet, patterned carpets and glowing candles.

Artistic invention

IN THE EARLY RENAISSANCE

As people became more interested in the world about them, in making images more lifelike, in learning and education, and in showing pride in their achievements, many artists became particularly inventive.

★

MAKING 2D LOOK 3D

An important aspect of making lifelike paintings and drawings was to try to make them look 3D. In about 1413, Filippo Brunelleschi (1377–1446), a Florentine architect, worked out the science and mathematics of linear perspective, or how to make paintings and drawings appear to have depth, space and distance. A few years later, the author and architect Leon Battista Alberti (1404–72) wrote a painting manual including information about **perspective**.

PERSPECTIVE LINES

Piero della Francesca, Masaccio and Paolo Uccello (1397–1475) were some of the first artists to use linear perspective in their paintings. Uccello was supposedly so keen on it that he often stayed up all night working out how to do it! In his painting *The Battle of San Romano*, he placed spears, lances and fallen men at angles to give viewers the feeling that they are looking right into the scene.

Saint George and the Dragon, Paolo Uccello, c.1470, oil on canvas, The National Gallery, London, UK. Uccello used lines and patches of grass to show his understanding of perspective.

*The Battle of San Romano,
Paolo Uccello, c.1438–40, egg
tempera with walnut oil and
linseed oil on poplar, The
National Gallery, London, UK.
Some of Uccello's perspective
is not quite right. Look at the
tiny fallen soldier on the left!*

*Dome of Florence Cathedral
(Santa Maria del Fiore), Filippo
Brunelleschi, 1420–36, brick and
wood, Florence, Italy.*

PRINTING BOOKS

Until the 1450s, books took ages to make and were expensive to produce, as most had to be written by hand. Around 1450, Johannes Gutenberg (c.1398–1468) invented a system of 'moveable type', which was made up of metal letters, symbols and numbers that could be moved and inked then printed to make thousands of books easily and more cheaply.

BRUNELLESCHI'S DOME

Brunelleschi was considered the first Renaissance architect. Between 1419 and 1436, he designed and built the huge dome on the cathedral of Florence using unique methods. It was the largest dome built since the Pantheon in ancient Rome, 1,500 years earlier.

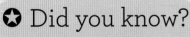

*One copy of The
Gutenberg Bible,
printed by Johannes
Gutenberg, 1454–5. This first printed
Bible was a lot less expensive than
handwritten books.*

⭐ Did you know?

Over four million bricks were used in the construction of Brunelleschi's dome. To build it, he also had to invent new ways of lifting heavy objects high into the air, which were used later by other architects.

THE INFORMATION REVOLUTION

An early wooden printing press such as Gutenberg's could produce up to 240 impressions per hour. Before this, handwritten manuscripts could take years to make. His invention changed history – the availability of books meant that more people could learn to read and become educated. His most famous book was a Bible that he produced in about 1454. It is not known how many copies he printed, but it was a bestseller!

Investigations and inventions

THE HIGH RENAISSANCE

By the 16th century, the Italian Renaissance was flourishing. Paintings showing tones, perspective and emotions, and sculpture conveying muscles and textures, were all becoming increasingly lifelike.

FROM FLORENCE TO ROME

As Italian painters began using oil paint, they created more tones and more vibrant colours. Encouraged by rich and powerful patrons, they began producing even larger and more impressive works of art. While Florence was at the heart of the early Renaissance, by the time of the High Renaissance focus had shifted to Rome and the Papal Court (the Popes who paid a lot of money for artwork). High Renaissance artists included Leonardo da Vinci (1452–1519), Michelangelo (1475–1564), Raphael (1483–1520), Correggio (1489–1534) and Titian (c.1485/90–1576).

⭐ Did you know?

The three greatest artists of the High Renaissance were Leonardo, Michelangelo and Raphael. Michelangelo disliked the younger Raphael and accused him of copying, but so did all artists! Raphael turned what he learnt into his own style.

CUTTING UP THE DEAD

Leonardo da Vinci is famed as a genius, one of the most gifted artists of all time, as well as an inventor. Rather than just accepting what things looked like, Leonardo wanted to understand what made everything work and how our eyes work when they see things. He experimented with light and shadow, and how light falls over objects, and he also got permission to dissect bodies and study them in the local hospitals (something usually only doctors needed to do).

Christ taking Leave of his Mother, Correggio, probably before 1514, oil on canvas, The National Gallery, London, UK.

Leonardo famously filled his sketchbooks with drawings and notes, all helping him to become a better artist. Fill your own sketchbook with drawings, photos, notes – explore your creativity! Left-handed Leonardo made all his notes in back-to-front, or mirror, writing, so they are not easy to decipher.

(Above) *The Virgin of the Rocks*, Leonardo da Vinci, c.1491/2–99 and 1506–8, oil on poplar, The National Gallery, London, UK.

(Left) *The Mona Lisa*, Leonardo da Vinci, c.1503–6, oil on poplar, Musée du Louvre, Paris, France.

RAPHAEL

One of the three most important High Renaissance artists, Raphael quickly picked up new ideas and techniques, and he was able to work on many different projects at once. The delicate and natural painting style of his figures and portraits made him famous during his short life.

RENAISSANCE MAN

Leonardo could draw and paint from an early age. He was also a great musician and invented things like weapons, a flying machine, a submarine and watermills, all far in advance of his time. Because he was clever in many different areas, he is often nicknamed 'the Renaissance Man'. His engineering and scientific inventions were ingenious and he also invented a method of shading, later called **sfumato**, which is a soft, almost smoky way of depicting outlines. This can be seen in *Mona Lisa*, c.1503–6, the most famous painting in the world, and in the two versions of *The Virgin of the Rocks*, c.1491/2–99 and 1506–8.

The Procession to Calvary, Raphael, c.1504–5, oil on poplar, The National Gallery, London, UK.

Michelangelo

One of the three greatest Italian Renaissance artists, and possibly the most influential artist in history, Michelangelo was nicknamed 'Il Divino' or 'The Divine One' for his extraordinarily powerful art. Exceptionally gifted, he was a painter, sculptor, architect, poet and engineer.

The Manchester Madonna,
Michelangelo, c.1497, tempera on wood,
The National Gallery, London, UK. An
unfinished painting by Michelangelo.

THE POPE'S CEILING

At that time, one of the most powerful people in the world was the Pope. In 1508 Pope Julius II (reigned 1503–13) asked Michelangelo to paint the huge ceiling of the Sistine Chapel in the Vatican in Rome. Over more than four years, Michelangelo painted nine scenes from the Old Testament high on the ceiling. He created nearly 300 figures in different poses, all with strong, muscular bodies, as he, like Leonardo, studied dead bodies in order to become a better artist. The bright colours, lively gestures and range of tones make the biblical stories seem vivid and real. Later on, he also painted *The Last Judgement* on the altar wall of the chapel. During the last years of his life, Michelangelo designed St Peter's Basilica in Rome which was being rebuilt, including the great dome, although he died before it was finished.

MAKING ARTISTS IMPORTANT

Because his genius was recognized during his lifetime, Michelangelo raised the status of artists, gave artists fresh ideas, and as a sign of how highly he was thought of, was given a purple cloak to swish around town in. Overall, he was a bit of a celebrity.

Part of the Sistine Chapel ceiling, Michelangelo, 1508–12, buon fresco, Vatican City, Italy.

SYMBOL OF FLORENCE

Born near Florence, Michelangelo began training as an artist when he was about 13 and initially learned fresco painting techniques. He showed an early talent in drawing and painting, but he always insisted that he was a sculptor first. One of his first sculptures was *Pietà* in Rome, a life-sized statue of Jesus after he was crucified being held by his mother Mary. Carved from a single block of marble, the sculpture shows his skills and understanding of the human figure.

As his fame as a great artist began to grow, he returned to Florence and received another commission to create a large statue of David from the biblical story David and Goliath. For two years he worked in secrecy, not letting anyone see his sculpture until it was finished. It was intended for the Cathedral, but when everyone saw it, it was decided to place it in the Piazza della Signoria as a reminder of the importance of the struggle against the enemies of Florence.

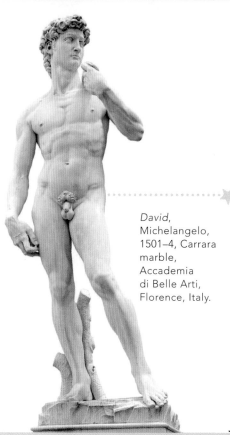

David, Michelangelo, 1501–4, Carrara marble, Accademia di Belle Arti, Florence, Italy.

Colourful stories

RENAISSANCE VENICE

Another of the largest and richest cities in Europe was Venice, a seaport on the east coast of Italy. Built on hundreds of tiny islands, Venice had grown rich, as sailors could travel easily from there and trade with other countries.

WORLD FAMOUS

Wealthy Venetian merchants liked to spend money on art, and Venice soon became world famous for the high quality of art and literature being produced there. The demand for art from both local and international patrons encouraged competition between artists which inspired new painting ideas. Venetian painters became known for the ways they layered and blended paints to achieve rich colours and for their 'painterly' technique where they worked directly onto the canvas without underdrawing.

TITIAN

The greatest Venetian artist of the Renaissance was Titian (c.1485/90–1576). He mixed many Renaissance ideas and created radiant colours, natural effects and dynamic compositions sometimes with lively brushwork. Among his patrons were prosperous Venetians, powerful families across Italy, kings of Spain and France, the Pope and the Holy Roman Emperor. From a young age he learned to make mosaics, then studied with Giovanni Bellini, and worked alongside Giorgione, all of whom influenced him. He painted many types of pictures and created lifelike portraits and compositions that seem full of life.

Bacchus and Ariadne, Titian, 1520–3, oil on canvas, The National Gallery, London, UK. Lively and colourful, Titian's paintings are full of people and energy.

Venetian Renaissance artists became known for the ways they used colour and brushmarks to suggest movement. Look closely at the paintings on these two pages and see how the artists created lively pictures, then paint your own dynamic and colourful picture using some of their techniques.

Allegory of Love: Happy Union, Veronese, c.1575, oil on canvas, The National Gallery, London, UK.

TINTORETTO AND VERONESE

Paolo Cagliari, or Veronese (1528–88), was another great Venetian artist of the High Renaissance. Also influenced by Michelangelo and Titian, he produced paintings using a sumptuous palette of colours. Jacopo Robusti, or Tintoretto (1518–94), produced inventive, animated and strikingly dramatic paintings. Although influenced by Titian and Michelangelo, he is usually described as a Mannerist (see pages 38–39). After Titian's death, Tintoretto and Veronese became the most important painters in Venice.

Saint George and the Dragon, Tintoretto, c.1555, oil on canvas, The National Gallery, London, UK.

BELLINI AND GIORGIONE

Giovanni Bellini (c.1413–1516) was one of the first Italian artists to use oil paints, and he painted large-scale altarpieces and smaller paintings in glowing colours and soft tones. His two best pupils were Giorgione (c.1477/78–1510) and Titian. Although little is known of Giorgione's life, and only six or seven paintings are signed by him, his small paintings are full of colour, dramatic light and atmosphere.

Close to nature

THE HIGH RENAISSANCE IN NORTHERN EUROPE

The impact of the Italian Renaissance reached northern Europe quickly, as several northern artists travelled to Italy and spent months – or sometimes years – there, studying artists' techniques, themes and materials. When they returned home, they tried out the new ideas and inspired others, but northern artists' art was always different from the work being produced in Italy.

★

ART PRINTS

The printing press was another way that ideas were spread across Europe. Thanks to Gutenberg's invention, **etchings** and engravings had become widely available, as well as books, and many people across Europe were buying engraved copies of contemporary Italian art.

STUDYING THE WORLD

Three of the greatest High Renaissance artists in northern Europe came from Germany – Albrecht Dürer (1471–1528), Matthias Grünewald (c.1475–1528) and Hans Holbein the Younger (c.1497–1543). Dürer travelled to Italy in 1494 and again in 1505. He met Giovanni Bellini and studied the work of other artists, including that of Leonardo and Andrea Mantegna (1431–1506). Skilled in drawing, watercolour painting, oil painting and copper engraving, Dürer's intense, lively and detailed style was particularly effective in prints – and these helped to spread his fame.

Saint Jerome, Albrecht Dürer, about 1496, oil on pearwood, The National Gallery, London, UK. This small painting shows Dürer's realistic style.

Hans Holbein's large double portrait, *The Ambassadors*, contains many symbols. On the furniture behind the two men, books, globes, musical instruments and other objects show how they were educated and knowledgeable about the world around them. The weird shape on the floor is a distorted human skull that can be seen 'properly' from one angle. It is a reminder that no one should become too pleased with themselves as we are all going to die eventually, and it is also an example of an artist showing off his skills!

A Young Princess (Dorothea of Denmark?), Jan Gossaert, c.1530, oil on oak, The National Gallery, London, UK. In a dress adorned with pearls, the princess holds an armillary sphere, a model of objects in the sky, symbolizing where she comes from.

The Ambassadors, Hans Holbein the Younger, 1533, oil on oak, The National Gallery, London, UK.

ATTENTION TO DETAIL

Matthias Grünewald was an intense visionary painter who made religious works, such as the extraordinary Isenheim altar (completed 1515), full of powerful and expressive imagery. Later in his career he followed Martin Luther who was leading a revolt against Catholicism (see page 38). Lucas Cranach the Elder (1472–1553) was also German and followed the new religion. A leading painter and printmaker, he focused on intricate details and painted several portraits of Luther. Hans Holbein the Younger became admired for his clear, precise portraits. He lived in England and painted for Henry VIII.

Rather stylish
MANNERISM

For hundreds of years, European artists simply accepted that their main job was to create religious images. Then from around 1520, arguments about religion made them all think again. Some people think that the exaggerations, distortions and tensions in Mannerism reflect the turbulence of society at a time of religious and political upheaval. Others see it as a style that was best suited to the wealthy courts of Europe with their skilful painters and sculptors, and increasingly demanding and intellectual patrons.

Allegory with Venus and Cupid, Bronzino, c.1545, oil on wood, The National Gallery, London, UK.

DISTORTING PROPORTIONS

Some artists copied Michelangelo's late painting style, and then distorted the proportions. Much later, and long after these artists had died, this style was nicknamed Mannerism, after the Italian word 'maniera' which means style. Meanwhile, many people of northern Europe were considering the ideas of the Reformation and the new Protestant culture did not allow art in their churches.

LIVELY STATUES

Giambologna (1529–1608) was a **Flemish** sculptor who moved to Italy and worked for the Medici family. His animated, elegant marble and bronze statues captured lively and dramatic stories and legends, and demonstrated incredible skill and daring in their execution.

THE REFORMATION

Martin Luther and his followers protested that Catholicism (the main religion of Europe at the time) had become too extravagant. They believed, among other things, that money being spent on art should be used to help the poor. The protesters became known as Protestants and the period came to be called the Reformation after the calls for reform in the Church.

The Madonna and Child with Saints, Moretto da Brescia, c.1540–5, oil on canvas, The National Gallery, London, UK.

THE MAIN MANNERISTS

One of the earliest Italian Mannerist painters was Pontormo (1494–1557), who became famous for his twisted poses, dramatic light and for teaching Bronzino (1503–72). Bronzino became famous for his technically perfect, elegant portraits and mythical scenes in brilliant, unnatural colours. Like Pontormo, Rosso Fiorentino (1494–1540) was one of the first Mannerists, who painted dramatic portraits and religious paintings. Parmigianino (1503–40) also became known for his portraits, but later even more for his exaggerated, long slim figures. One of his paintings is now known as *The Madonna with the Long Neck*! In Spain, El Greco (1541–1614) used long thin figures and expressive colours to suggest religious intensity in his paintings.

(Above Left) *Joseph with Jacob in Egypt*, Pontormo, probably 1518, oil on wood, The National Gallery, London, UK.

(Above) *The Madonna with the Long Neck*, detail, Parmigianino, c.1535, oil on wood, Uffizi Gallery, Florence, Italy.

(Below) *Portrait of Three Children*, Marietta Robusti, 1575–90, oil on canvas, Pinacoteca Ambrosiana, Milan, Italy. Marietta was Tintoretto's daughter, often called Tintoretta.

✪ Did you know?

In the 16th century, there were some young women being taught to paint by their artist fathers – at a time when most women were expected to marry or join a convent. Although it was difficult for them, some were successful, including Lavinia Fontana (1552–1614), Barbara Longhi (1552–1638) and Marietta Robusti (c.1554–90) – Tintoretto's daughter.

High drama
THE BAROQUE

While Renaissance art had recreated ancient Roman styles and harmonious, lifelike portraits, myths and Bible stories, **Baroque** art was far more dramatic.

DRAMA AND DYNAMISM

Baroque comes from the Portuguese word 'barocco' meaning misshapen pearl, and was used later to describe the movement that mixed emotions, dynamism and drama. This new art was an attempt by the Catholic Church to strengthen its image and to show Protestants its power. The period became known as the Counter-Reformation, and artists portrayed Bible stories in as exciting ways as they could to encourage followers back into the Catholic Church.

LOOKING UP

One of the first Baroque painters, Annibale Carracci (1560–1609), began painting energetic and naturalistic pictures but became more **classical** when he moved to Rome. Across the vast ceiling of the Palazzo Farnese in Rome, he painted pictures showing stories from the life of Hercules.

The Ecstasy of Saint Teresa, Gianlorenzo Bernini, 1647–52, marble, Santa Maria della Vittoria, Rome, Italy.

EMOTION AND EXPRESSION

Gianlorenzo Bernini (1598–1680) was an amazing Baroque sculptor who could make cold, hard marble look soft and warm. His figures have dramatic, emotional expressions and he gave then a sense of movement.

Boy Bitten by a Lizard, Caravaggio, 1595–1600, oil on canvas, The National Gallery, London, UK. Caravaggio's strong contrasting of light and dark is called 'chiaroscuro' or 'tenebrism'.

CHIAROSCURO

Although Baroque artists had similarities, they also had individual ideas. Caravaggio (1571–1610) created a **revolution** in painting. He portrayed religious figures as poor, sometimes ugly people, rather than refined and beautiful, which was shocking at the time. Sometimes the dirty feet or fingernails of the figures were clearly visible to the viewers. He painted dramatic, dark compositions full of emotional tension, with concentrated areas of light. This is called '**chiaroscuro**', from the Italian words 'chiaro', meaning light, and 'scuro', meaning dark.

POWERFUL WOMEN

In an era that was difficult for female artists, Artemisia Gentileschi (1593–c.1656) painted dramatic pictures in strong chiaroscuro, mainly of powerful women from myths and the Bible.

Jael and Sisera, Artemisia Gentileschi, c.1620, oil on canvas, Museum of Fine Arts, Budapest, Hungary.

★ **Did you know?**

Caravaggio killed a man in a brawl. He was later pardoned for the murder, but many people never forgave him for making holy figures look poor and scruffy.

SPAIN

Diego Velázquez (1599–1660) is often described as the most important painter of the Spanish Baroque. His original, fluid painting technique with light brushstrokes and suggested highlights broke with tradition, and the King of Spain loved his work. He painted some of the greatest portraits of the Spanish court.

The Holy Family with the Infant Saint John the Baptist, Annibale Carracci, c.1600, oil on copper, The National Gallery, London, UK.

Philip IV of Spain in Brown and Silver, detail, Diego Velázquez, c.1631–32, oil on canvas, The National Gallery, London, UK.

The Dutch golden age

While Catholic countries encouraged art that celebrated their beliefs, most Protestant countries banned religious art. Instead of large, colourful altarpieces Protestant churches had plain white walls. But in Holland people still liked to have small religious pictures at home, so some Dutch artists painted homely scenes with religious or moral messages.

★

REAL LIFE

As there was no longer such a market for religious paintings, Dutch painters began producing more landscapes, **still lifes**, outdoor and indoor scenes, and portraits – all pictures of everyday life.

✪ Did you know?

Vermeer may have used a special lens to help him make his pictures. It projected what he was drawing on to a wall.

LIGHT ON LIFE

Jan – or Johannes – Vermeer (1632–75) specialized in painting interiors of affluent households. Making daily life his subjects, his meticulous paintings are filled with lustrous light because of the way he applied paint in dappled highlights. Jan Steen (c.1626–79) painted amusing pictures of everyday life (usually bad behaviour!), featuring hidden meanings that pointed out morals – or right from wrong.

Young Woman Seated at a Virginal, Johannes Vermeer, c.1670–2, oil on canvas, The National Gallery, London, UK.

A Still Life of Flowers in a Wan-Li Vase, Ambrosius Bosschaert the Elder, 1609–10, oil on copper, The National Gallery, London, UK.

STAYING STILL

Still life painting – ordinary objects in arrangements – was quite a new idea. Dutch and Flemish artists became incredibly good at painting precise details of these, and flower paintings, as personal possessions and gardens suggested wealth. People were proud to own such pictures and they admired the artists' meticulous skills. Some of the most skilful were: Rachel Ruysch (1664–1750), famous for her flower paintings; Ambrosius Bosschaert the Elder (1573–1621), known for his detailed still lifes with flowers; and Jan de Heem (c.1606–83/4), who painted elaborate goblets, platters, flowers and fruit.

A Road Winding between Trees towards a Distant Cottage, Jacob van Ruisdael, c.1645–50, oil on oak, The National Gallery, London, UK.

PAINTING PEOPLE

Frans Hals (c.1582–1666) was a great portrait painter who used loose brushwork (a style often called 'painterly') and helped to introduce a lively style of painting into Dutch art.

LANDSCAPES

One of the most famous landscape painters of 17th-century Holland was Jacob van Ruisdael (1628/9–82) who painted realistic views with cool blue, green and brown tones to suggest the 'northern' atmosphere. Paintings of towns and the countryside appealed to Dutch pride in their country and you can often spot the windmills in the background.

REMINDERS OF DEATH

Some Dutch still life arrangements were deliberately selected to remind viewers that we are all going to die, so no one should become too proud or greedy. Called '**vanitas**' paintings, sometimes they included skulls and other symbols of death, such as hourglasses or burning candles, or objects that showed self-indulgence, such as jewellery or playing cards.

Still Life: An Allegory of the Vanities of Human Life, Harmen Steenwyck, c.1640, oil on oak, The National Gallery, London, UK.

Rembrandt

One of the greatest European artists ever, and the most important Dutch artist of the Baroque period, Rembrandt van Rijn (1606–69) demonstrated a talent for art from an early age. He spent most of his life in Amsterdam, which was one of the richest cities in Europe at that time, and full of wealthy merchants who were excited to buy his art.

IMAGINATION AND CURIOSITY

Rembrandt's imagination and curiosity led him to explore a far wider range of subjects than most other artists of the time. As he was from Protestant Holland, his biblical scenes were not painted for churches, but he used them to explore human emotions and reactions. His compassion and understanding of human nature meant that he painted all stories from unusual and sympathetic points of view.

Belshazzar's Feast, Rembrandt, c.1636–8, oil on canvas, The National Gallery, London, UK.

(Left) *Self-Portrait at the Age of 63*, Rembrandt, 1669, oil on canvas, The National Gallery, London, UK.

(Above) *Self-Portrait at the Age of 34*, Rembrandt, 1640, oil on canvas, The National Gallery, London, UK.

NEW IDEAS

During this period, that became known as the Dutch Golden Age, new ideas were tried out in art, particularly in painting. Rembrandt tried using soft colouring to create a mellow light and his chiaroscuro made his dynamic compositions seem especially dramatic. He was one of the first artists to apply sketchy, directional brushstrokes – making marks that followed the directions of objects he was painting. Later, he also often applied thick paint with a **palette knife**, so his paint marks were even more visible. This style was revolutionary, as traditionally painters were expected to make their brushmarks invisible, and create smooth finishes. The thick paint on many of Rembrandt's works is called '**impasto**'.

POWERFUL PORTRAITS

A master at painting, drawing and etching (a printing process), Rembrandt's scenes are dramatic and lively, often seeming to capture fleeting moments, while emphasizing feelings. He became best known for his powerful and moving portraits, of individuals, groups, and many of himself, that explored personalities and particularly himself as he aged. Over time, his portraits became more perceptive – he seemed to capture the characters of his subjects spontaneously, and he could paint natural-looking, busy crowd scenes with ease.

TRAGEDY AND HARDSHIP

Having been extremely successful during his early career and achieving fame and fortune, Rembrandt's home life became affected by tragedy and hardships. In the 1640s, his wife, Saskia, and his mother died. He became introverted and began painting more religious works. Ten years later, Amsterdam suffered a huge economic crisis and he lost all his money. By then his sketchier style was not liked as much and he struggled to gain commissions. In the 1660s, his partner Hendrijke and beloved son Titus also died.

Ecce Homo, Rembrandt, 1634, oil on paper mounted onto canvas, The National Gallery, London, UK.

Van Dyck

Anthony van Dyck (1599–1641) was an important Flemish painter, extremely successful in Italy, but best remembered for his elegant paintings of the English court of King Charles I, which influenced English portrait painting for the next 150 years.

RELAXED AND REFINED

Van Dyck's portraits are relaxed and refined, many with landscape backgrounds. He seemed to always capture the inner feelings and personalities that his subjects wanted to present, and his rendering of fabrics and other textures, from shiny silks and satins, to soft velvet, or frilly lace and flowing hair, attracted great admiration.

BEST PUPIL

A clever child, Van Dyck began training as an artist at the age of 10. Later, he became the chief assistant to the greatest Flemish artist, Peter Paul Rubens (1577–1640), who had a huge workshop. Master artists often allowed their assistants to finish off paintings or to paint areas of their own great works. As a teenager, Van Dyck was one of these, and Rubens described him as "the best of my pupils". Hugely influenced by Rubens, Van Dyck developed light, flowing brushstrokes, clever compositions and shimmering colours. He produced oil paintings, watercolours, engravings and etchings.

A Roman Triumph, Peter Paul Rubens, c.1630, oil on canvas mounted on oak, The National Gallery, London, UK.

Equestrian Portrait of Charles I, Anthony van Dyck, 1637–8, oil on canvas, The National Gallery, London, UK.

FIRST COURT PAINTER

In 1620, he travelled to London and worked for King James I, then from 1621 to 1627, he worked in Italy, painting portraits for the aristocracy. As a devout Catholic, his religious paintings were highly emotional, but after his successes in England and Italy, he began concentrating on painting portraits. After working in the Netherlands for five years, King Charles I and Queen Henrietta-Maria invited him back to England to be principal painter to the king. They gave him a house, a studio, money and a knighthood. His flattering and imposing portraits of Charles I and his family inspired other artists, both in England and beyond.

The Balbi Children, Anthony van Dyck, c.1625–7, oil on canvas, The National Gallery, London, UK.

KING CHARLES I

King Charles I was the most passionate art collector of British royalty there had been, and he believed that art would promote him as a grand and powerful monarch. After seeing the portrait of his sister, Queen Elizabeth of Bohemia, painted by Van Dyck in 1632, he immediately summoned the artist to London and paid him handsomely for his work. Instantly successful in England, Van Dyck produced many portraits of the royal family, some to be sent as gifts and some to adorn the royal palaces. In all, he painted about forty portraits of the King, and thirty of the Queen, as well as several of their children and courtiers.

French grandeur

In the 17th century, France was rising in power, with a population of 21 million, while Spain only had 7 million and Britain 5.5 million. The French royal court was powerful and extravagant, first under Louis XIII, and then under Louis XIV, who became known as the 'Sun King'.

★

EXTRAVAGANT AND GRAND

Although Baroque art and architecture had started in Rome, other European countries interpreted the ideas in different ways. Largely through Louis XIV's court in France, Baroque art and architecture became extravagant and grand, suggesting power and might.

The Finding of Moses, Nicolas Poussin, 1651, oil on canvas, The National Gallery, London, UK.

PAINTING PICTURES OF HISTORY

Nicolas Poussin (1594–1665) and Claude Lorrain (1600–82) were two of France's greatest Baroque painters and spent most of their careers in Rome. Except for a short time back in France working for the king, Poussin worked in Rome, painting stories from literature and the Bible in harmonious, clear compositions inspired by Titian, Raphael and ancient Roman art. Claude became one of the leading landscape painters of the period, creating idealized scenes with accurate perspective and beautiful atmospheric light.

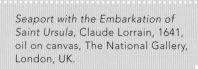

Seaport with the Embarkation of Saint Ursula, Claude Lorrain, 1641, oil on canvas, The National Gallery, London, UK.

DRAMATIC EFFECTS

Several French artists were influenced by Caravaggio, including Valentin de Boulogne (1591–1632) and Georges de la Tour (1593–1652). Both artists created dramatic chiaroscuro effects. Philippe de Champaigne (1602–74) became the leading French portrait painter of Louis XIII.

King Louis XIV of France dressed in the costume of the Sun King in the ballet *La Nuit*, French School, 1653, Bibliothèque Nationale, Paris, France.

Cardinal de Richelieu, Philippe de Champaigne, 1633–40, oil on canvas, The National Gallery, London, UK.

THE SUN KING

Louis XIV (who reigned from 1661 to 1715), became known as the Sun King because of the splendour of his court and the ways in which he used art and architecture to glorify his power. French kings ruled alone, with no parliament to balance their authority, and it was believed that they ruled 'by divine right' – which meant through God's choice. Louis thought everything should revolve around him (rather like the sun)!

VERSAILLES

In 1682, Louis XIV's opulent new palace, Versailles, became his official residence. As a symbol of his power and accomplishments, it had to show how magnificent he was. So he employed architects, sculptors and painters to decorate it lavishly. The Baroque style was perfect for such sumptuousness.

THE ACADEMY

In 1648, Louis XIV founded the French Academy of Painting and Sculpture, which ran its own school to train artists, had an exhibition each year (called **the Salon**), and decided on the 'official' art for France. It controlled everything about French art and so after it began, artists could usually only be successful if their work was chosen to be exhibited in the annual Salon.

Love in the air

THE ROCOCO

As a reaction against the drama of Baroque art and architecture, the **Rococo** began in the 18th century. This playful, light-hearted style first appeared in interior design, which was admired by artists and soon adapted and used in fine art as well.

★

FÊTES GALANTES

Rococo paintings often featured elegantly dressed people having fun in lush country surroundings. These light, frolicsome scenes became known as '**fêtes galantes**' (courtly parties). They were introduced by Watteau when he applied to join the French Academy in 1717. At that time, there was no suitable classification for his paintings, but academy officials liked his work, so rather than reject him, they created a new category for him – fêtes galantes. These were not just ordinary outdoor views, but seemed magical or mystical, with humans in heavenly surroundings, in harmony with nature.

BRIGHT AND WITTY

Leading Rococo painters included Giovanni Battista Tiepolo (1696–1770), Jean-Antoine Watteau (1684–1721), François Boucher (1703–70), Jean-Honoré Fragonard (1732–1806) and Jean-Baptiste-Siméon Chardin (1699–1779). Their bright, witty and sometimes mischievous paintings contrasted with the dramatic, serious and grand works of the Baroque.

❂ Did you know?

The movement was named the Rococo. The origin of the name is still debated. It possibly came from the French word 'rocaille', meaning a rock formation associated with water. The irregular patterns and shells of rocaille often appeared in Rococo decoration and art, and so became linked with the Rococo style.

The Scale of Love, Jean-Antoine Watteau, 1715–8, oil on canvas, The National Gallery, London, UK. This is one of Watteau's fêtes galantes.

PERSONAL PLEASURES

The fêtes galantes scenes of people enjoying themselves were well suited to this carefree and pretty style. Other Rococo subjects included mythological stories and portraits. In England, the style was described as 'French taste' and English artists who followed it tended to paint landscapes, portraits or witty pictures that mocked society.

Psyche Showing her Sisters her Gifts from Cupid, Jean-Honoré Fragonard, 1753, oil on canvas, The National Gallery, London, UK.

LOUIS XV

The Rococo movement began in France after the death of Louis XIV in 1715. The Sun King's heir was his five year old great-grandson. At first, the new king's great-uncle Philippe II, Duke of Orléans ruled as Regent, but from 1723, Louis XV took control of his kingdom. Throughout his reign, the French court was showy and extravagant, and the styles of the Rococo flourished. The King's favourite mistress, Madame de Pompadour, encouraged Rococo in architecture, decorative and fine art, and it remained in fashion until about 1750.

Marriage A-la-Mode: The Marriage Settlement, William Hogarth, c.1743, oil on canvas, The National Gallery, London, UK. Mocking the upper classes, this shows a marriage contract being made between a poor earl's son and a rich merchant's daughter.

Madame de Pompadour at Her Tambour Frame, François-Hubert Drouais, 1763–4, oil on canvas, The National Gallery, London, UK.

MADAME DE POMPADOUR

Madame de Pompadour allowed herself to be shown as a gentle, fashionable lady embroidering, surrounded by beautiful furniture, books, musical instruments and her playful little dog. But don't let the soft, gentle style of her dress and her sweet expression fool you! She was an extremely powerful woman who often met with people while she sewed and helped them arrange meetings with the King.

The floating city

VENICE AND ITS PAINTERS

During the 17th and 18th centuries, Venice became a popular tourist destination. It was common for rich young gentlemen and newly married couples to visit this 'floating city' while on European trips, which could last for five years! By the 1780s, as many as 40,000 tourists travelled to Venice each year.

Exhibition of a Rhinoceros at Venice, Pietro Longhi, c.1751, oil on canvas, The National Gallery, London, UK.

THE GRAND TOUR

From the early 17th century, it became fashionable for young aristocrats from England, Germany and Scandinavia to visit Paris, Venice, Florence and Rome to learn about history, literature, art, architecture and culture. They often travelled with tutors and guides and the trip became known as the 'Grand Tour'. At the end of each tour, the travellers took art objects and paintings home with them to remind them of their experiences.

Venice: The Grand Canal with San Simeone Piccolo, Canaletto, c.1740, oil on canvas, The National Gallery, London, UK. Canaletto's perfect perspective, glittering light and landmarks of Venice all appealed to tourists.

CARNEVALE

Carnival (or 'Carnevale') is one of the biggest celebrations in Venice. It began in the 12th century when people wanted to use up all their rich food and drink and have a party before the restrictions of Lent. By the 16th century, dressing up in fancy clothes and masks had become a tradition as well. Pietro Longhi (1701/2–85) painted everyday scenes around Venice. His picture *Exhibition of a Rhinoceros at Venice*, painted in about 1751, shows Clara the rhinoceros who was taken on a tour around Europe for ten years in the mid-18th century. One of the few rhinoceroses that had been seen in Europe, she became quite a celebrity!

Canaletto and Guardi's paintings of Venice emphasized certain aspects of the city to remind people of happy memories. Draw a picture of a place you have been on holiday – what will you make important in it?

Venice: Piazza San Marco, Francesco Guardi, about 1760, oil on canvas, The National Gallery, London, UK.

The Virgin and Child appearing to a Group of Saints, Giovanni Battista Tiepolo, c.1735, oil on canvas, The National Gallery, London, UK.

UNIQUE LIGHT

As part of the Grand Tour in Venice, travellers admired the paintings of Bellini, Giorgione, Titian and Veronese, made in the Renaissance period. They took in the architecture, surroundings and atmosphere, and they enjoyed the carnival season, travelling in gondolas and staying in grand palaces. Among their favourite souvenirs to take home as mementos were paintings of the city, especially those by Canaletto (1697–1768) and Francesco Guardi (1712–93). These paintings captured detailed views of the city and also depicted the unique light, canals and atmosphere of Venice.

TIEPOLO

Giovanni Battista Tiepolo was also Venetian and, inspired by Veronese, is often considered to be the greatest Italian Rococo painter. His happy paintings show lots of people from different viewpoints in luminous colours, rich textures, and curling lines.

Neoclassicism

At the end of the 18th century, there were revolutions in France and America as people fought for their beliefs of having fairer conditions for everyone. At the same time, new inventions and ideas in technology, science and the arts were developing, which changed the way that many people lived across Europe and America.

Whistlejacket, George Stubbs, c.1762, oil on canvas, The National Gallery, London, UK. Whistlejacket was a famous racehorse and his owner commissioned this painting.

REBELLION

In 1789, the French overthrew their king and all aristocrats who had been powerful simply because they were born rich. Between 1765 and 1783 in America, settlers fought their British rulers and declared their independence. These rebellions affected people across the world as everyone began to think about wealth and fairness. Many began challenging old traditions and demanding better opportunities for all. Neoclassical artists began painting dramatic scenes of history, myths or exciting events, to reflect all the new discoveries, developments and thinking.

Portrait of Jacobus Blauw, Jacques-Louis David, 1795, oil on canvas, The National Gallery, London, UK. From the Dutch Republic, the judge, politician and diplomat Blauw helped establish the Batavian Republic in Holland. David has painted him looking powerful.

THE ENLIGHTENMENT

As part of these new developments, people were becoming more educated. Many scientists and philosophers began thinking in new ways, much as people had done during the Renaissance. Some of the leading intellectuals included Sir Isaac Newton (1643–1727), Montesquieu (1689–1755), Voltaire (1694–1778), Denis Diderot (1713–84) and Jean-Jacques Rousseau (1712–78). Scientists also began looking closely at animals – George Stubbs (1724–1806) published a book called *The Anatomy of the Horse* in 1766. These clever thinkers wanted to work out many of the mysteries of the universe. This period was later called The Enlightenment.

Make a Neoclassical picture!
Draw someone you know next
to or holding an object. Draw
your outlines carefully and shade
gently with a range of tones to
make your picture look 3D, like
a Neoclassical work of art.

The Three Graces, Antonio Canova, 1814–17,
marble, Victoria and Albert Museum, London, UK.

*An Experiment on a Bird in an Air
Pump*, Joseph Wright of Derby,
1768, oil on canvas, The National
Gallery, London, UK. Strong
chiaroscuro emphasizes the action
of this painting.

STUDYING THE WORLD

New ideas about investigating the world are shown
in the art of Joseph Wright of Derby (1734–97),
who was fascinated by new scientific discoveries.
His painting *Experiment on a Bird in an Air Pump*
shows a family around a table, watching a travelling
scientist demonstrating different ideas about the
creation of a vacuum and encouraging the family
to think about how their world works.

EXCAVATIONS

In the mid-1700s, two discoveries were made in
southern Italy. Two ancient Roman towns were
found buried beneath the ground. In 79 CE, a
huge volcanic eruption covered Herculaneum and
Pompeii with lava. Everyone was killed, but all
the buildings and art treasures were preserved by
the ash! As the towns were uncovered in the 18th
century, people learned a lot about how the ancient
Romans had lived. The discoveries helped to inspire
a new **art movement** that followed styles of classical
Rome and Greece. It was later called **Neoclassicism**
('New Classicism'). Some of the best Neoclassical
artists were Jacques-Louis David (1748–1825), Jean-
Auguste-Dominique Ingres (1780–1867) and sculptor
Antonio Canova (1757–1822).

Big on emotion

THE ROMANTICS

As well as The Enlightenment, the revolutions in America and France aroused strong emotions, particularly when the great ideals didn't always match the realities. Some artists and writers began expressing this in literature, painting and sculpture – at the same time as Neoclassical art was being made.

★

Doña Isabel de Porcel, Francisco de Goya, before 1805, The National Gallery, London, UK.

BOLD COLOURS

The new, emotional style of art came to be called **Romanticism**. The artists wanted to express feelings, drama and the power of nature. While Neoclassical artists were careful to draw precise, clean lines with cool tonal contrasts, Romantic artists expressed themselves through bold colour, sweeping brushstrokes and dramatic lighting.

DRAMA AND PASSION

Deep passions were stirred by fighting. Francisco de Goya (1746–1816), a court painter to the Spanish king, painted portraits and religious and historical works. When his country was invaded by the new French emperor, Napoleon I, he protested about the horrors of war in expressive and intensely coloured paintings. Eugène Delacroix (1798–1863) and Théodore Géricault (1791–1824), two of the most famous Romantic painters, created spectacular, dramatic, action-filled paintings, emphasizing emotion and using colour to rouse strong feelings in viewers.

The Execution of Lady Jane Grey, Paul Delaroche, 1833, oil on canvas, The National Gallery, London, UK.

Ovid among the Scythians, Eugène Delacroix, 1859, oil on canvas, The National Gallery, London, UK.

Winter Landscape, Caspar David Friedrich, probably 1811, oil on canvas, The National Gallery, London, UK.

ATMOSPHERIC IMAGES

Caspar David Friedrich (1774–1840) was a great landscape painter of the time whose atmospheric paintings are full of a mystical sense of God's grandeur.

NATURE'S POWER

Some Romantic painters believed that nature could – and should – affect people's moods. They thought that landscapes could be calm and beautiful, or awe-inspiring and powerful and they aimed to show this in paint. Rather than only painting in their studios, some of these artists began making oil sketches outdoors, which was tricky at this time as paint was difficult to carry. John Constable (1775–1837) spent hours painting oil sketches outside, capturing images of landscapes which he then reworked in his studio. He used dabs and flecks of paint to convey his vision of trees, water and clouds and create a sense of the weather and atmosphere.

The Hay Wain, John Constable, 1821, oil on canvas, The National Gallery, London, UK.

Turner

During the Romantic era, the Industrial Revolution was changing how people lived. Machines meant that factories could efficiently and cheaply produce many goods, while trains had begun to travel through towns and cities that were growing larger and busier.

LIGHT AND WEATHER EFFECTS

Although Joseph Mallord William Turner (1775–1851) was fascinated by nature, he also marvelled at the new machines and how they were affecting the world. He produced hundreds of spectacular paintings and was the most famous English landscape painter of the Romantic movement. His early style was influenced by past masters, such as Claude Lorrain, but his later pioneering paintings of light, atmosphere and weather effects inspired many artists who followed him.

Calais Pier, J.M.W. Turner, 1803, oil on canvas, The National Gallery, London, UK. Storm clouds and a wild sea dominate the scene, which Turner painted from a real-life event.

The Fighting Temeraire, J.M.W. Turner, 1839, oil on canvas, The National Gallery, London, UK. With lively brushmarks and bold colours for the sunset, Turner created an atmospheric scene.

EXHILARATING VIEWS

Turner's exhilarating views of mountains, the sea, buildings and ships were revolutionary for the time, but by leaving out details in order to capture the overall atmosphere of each scene, he annoyed some of his contemporaries who thought that good art should be precise and lifelike. Look back to page 6 and see what he said when someone criticized his work!

EXPRESSIVE BRUSHSTROKES

As well as exploring and painting enthusiastically around the British Isles, Turner often travelled abroad to find breathtaking scenes and to gather new ideas. His painting style became looser and more energetic as he tried to capture exciting illusions of what he saw. After 1830, he applied his paint in many unusual ways to achieve his effects, with brushes, rags or palette knives, and thick and thin textures. Often he lightened his canvases with a layer of white paint before applying unexpected colours with expressive marks.

Rain, Steam and Speed – The Great Western Railway, J.M.W. Turner, 1844, oil on canvas, The National Gallery, London, UK.

A WILD NATURE

Turner worked in oils and watercolours, and he also produced engravings which sold well, so his art became known more widely. His fresh approach, bright colours and way of making light seem to dissolve eventually brought him fame. Many of his dramatic paintings show the land or sea, but they are really his way of showing the strength, beauty and wildness of nature, such as can be seen in sunsets and storms. Some of his pictures reveal humans trying to battle against nature's power and unpredictability, and some show ancient landscapes being transformed by human invention, such as new steamships and trains. Most of all, he concentrated on the effects of light – and his work laid the foundations for several later art movements.

Landscape and Realism

By the mid-1800s, the Western world was changing even more speedily than it had been earlier in the century, as new machines and inventions were created.

★

THE ORDINARY WORLD

The art movement became known as 'Realism' and from the 1840s, it lasted for over thirty years. Showing the ordinary world deliberately contrasted with Neoclassicism and Romanticism. Realists were not interested in depicting royalty or rich and powerful figures. People in their paintings did not look wealthy, beautiful or fashionable, and landscapes had no symbolism or sensational effects.

A DIRECT APPROACH

With factories and railway lines changing the countryside, and poor people's lives not improving, several artists chose to paint exactly what they saw, just the real world, directly with no fancy stories or spectacular compositions. These artists intended to make society think about life as it really was, especially for poor people.

Don Quixote and Sancho Panza, Honoré-Victorin Daumier, c.1855, oil on canvas, The National Gallery, London, UK.

SQUEEZABLE PAINTS

Before the 1840s, it was difficult for artists to paint outdoors. The first ready-made paint was sold in pig's bladders. They had to be pierced and then sealed with a tack. Then, in 1841, the American portrait painter John Goffe Rand (1801–73) invented squeezable metal tubes. At last, artists could paint wherever they wanted.

The Winnower, Jean-François Millet, c.1847–8, oil on canvas, The National Gallery, London, UK.

PHOTOGRAPHY

In 1839, photography was invented. Its impact on
painters was enormous. Once people could take
photographs (even though at first they were only black
and white and were awkward to develop), many artists
believed that no one would want paintings any more.
Others decided that photography could help them plan
compositions and capture lifelike, believable scenes.

THE BARBIZON SCHOOL

With newly portable paints, more artists painted away
from their studios. In the mid-1840s, a group of French
artists began painting in the Forest of Fontainebleau.
They painted from direct observation, just the views
they saw in front of them. They called themselves the
Barbizon School after the village they stayed in.

✪ Did you know?

Rosa Bonheur (1822–99) overcame
prejudices about female artists and
became a famous Realist, particularly
known for her lively, light-filled paintings
of animals and the countryside.

PEASANT PAINTINGS

One of the main Realist painters was Gustave Courbet
(1819–77), who painted poor people working, as well
as landscapes and seascapes. Using a palette knife,
he built up small dabs of colour across his canvases.
Jean-François Millet (1814–75) also understood the
hardships caused by poverty and painted peasants at
work, looking tired but dignified. He used unexpected
bright colours, creating softly glowing effects.

Beach Scene, Gustave Courbet, 1874,
oil on canvas, The National Gallery,
London, UK. One of the main Realists,
Courbet painted what he saw directly
on to his canvases.

Representing modern life

Often described as the first modern painter, Édouard Manet (1832–83), painted sketchy pictures of contemporary people and life. At first, his work was considered outrageous and shocking, but he later became appreciated and his influence on other artists was huge.

BROAD BRUSHWORK

Manet came from a wealthy background, he wore stylish, fashionable clothes, and he really wanted to gain the official French Academy's approval for his art. Inspired by Velázquez and Goya, his early work was dramatic and bold, but then he began painting scenes of everyday life using strong colours and broad brushwork. These works contrasted with traditional art, yet he was still upset when the Academy rejected his paintings.

Corner of a Café-Concert, Édouard Manet, c.1878–80, oil on canvas, The National Gallery, London, UK. Manet's subjects and style were greatly inspired by Goya.

IMPRESSIONIST FRIENDS

Although Manet received much criticism, the **Impressionists** (see pages 64–65) admired his work, and he became good friends with several of them, particularly Claude Monet (1840–1926) and Edgar Degas (1834–1917). His paintings became more impressionistic in style, but he never joined in their exhibitions, as he always wanted to exhibit in the more traditional setting of the French Salon. Eventually, in the 1870s, his work began to be acclaimed. Several paintings were accepted by the Salon and he even received a medal in 1881.

MODERN SCULPTURE

Another artist of the time who was friends with the Impressionists was the sculptor Auguste Rodin (1840–1917). His work was also rejected by the Academy, but by the time he died, he was being compared to Michelangelo, and is now recognized as 'the father of modern sculpture'. Unlike many sculptors of the time, he never created statues of gods, but made lifelike statues of ordinary, modern people.

The Thinker, Auguste Rodin, 1879–89, bronze, The Metropolitan Museum of Art, New York, USA.

Art Lesson

Make a chalk pastel picture like Degas. It's an art material you can smudge with your fingers! Draw your picture using light lines and instead of black for dark areas, use dark blue or brown. Notice how many colours Degas used, and blend the colours with your fingers as he did.

After the Bath, Woman Drying Herself, Edgar Degas, c.1890–5, pastel on paper on board, The National Gallery, London, UK.

Miss La La at the Cirque Fernando, Edgar Degas, 1879, oil on canvas, The National Gallery, London, UK.

PICTURES LIKE PHOTOGRAPHS

Degas was one of the leading Impressionists, who created paintings, sculptures, prints and drawings. An admirer of Ingres and Delacroix, and greatly influenced by Manet, he soon began depicting people and modern life. He used photographs to help him create unusual compositions that drew viewers right into the action of his pictures and to make them appear like casual moments. His favourite subjects included ballet dancers, women washing and horses and horse racing.

Impressionism

Impressionism was a revolution in art! It was inspired by several things, including Realism and Barbizon paintings, photography and portable paints, Turner's effects, people's changing lifestyles, and Manet. The most famous Impressionists are Degas, Monet (1840–1926), Auguste Renoir (1841–1919) and Camille Pissarro (1830–1903).

MESSY AND UNFINISHED

The Impressionists went against traditions and painted everyday life in sketchy, colourful ways. As cameras could now capture accurate likenesses, Impressionists decided that painters should do something different. This angered many who liked precise painting. French Academy officials scoffed at their work and refused to exhibit their paintings in the annual Salon, believing that they looked messy and unfinished, and that the artists had no skill.

EN PLEIN AIR

Once ready-made paint in tubes began to be manufactured, artists could work outside easily. Aiming to capture changing light and weather conditions, the Impressionists painted completed, finished works 'en plein air' (in the open air), using paint tubes and new portable box easels that carried paints, then unfolded to become easels to paint on.

Art Lesson

Several new scientific theories about colour excited the Impressionists. One stated that colours opposite each other on the **colour wheel** – called **complementary colours** – appear brighter if next to each other. **Primary colours** are red, blue and yellow. **Secondary colours** are purple (red + blue), green (blue + yellow) and orange (red + yellow). When you mix a primary with a secondary colour, or two secondary colours, you create **tertiary colours**.

Orange

Yellow

Green

Blue

Hélène Rouart in her Father's Study, Edgar Degas, c.1886, oil on canvas, The National Gallery, London, UK. Degas used complementary colours across this painting.

At the Theatre (La Première Sortie), Auguste Renoir, 1876–7, oil on canvas, The National Gallery, London, UK.

MOMENTS IN TIME

The Impressionists painted pictures that captured fleeting moments in time without detail. They were more concerned with light and colour than with showing details. To save time, they used rapid brushstrokes and often unmixed colours. Frequently choosing unusual viewpoints, they painted landscapes, views of city streets and scenes of people relaxing, such as in cafés, theatres, dance halls, in their gardens or at the seaside.

INDEPENDENT EXHIBITIONS

The Impressionists all lived in Paris and knew Manet, who had been criticized for his paintings of modern life, ordinary people and places, made quickly with patches of colour rather than smooth, careful layers. The Impressionists admired his style and subject matter, and used it in their paintings. In 1874, fed up with their Salon rejections, they set up their own exhibition. One painting exhibited by Monet was of a misty harbour, called *Impression: Sunrise*. A critic writing about the exhibition insultingly called all the art 'impressions' after Monet's painting.

Summer's Day, Berthe Morisot, c.1879, oil on canvas, The National Gallery, London, UK.

Monet

As well as one of his paintings giving Impressionism its name, Claude Monet is often recognized as the leader of the movement. Rejecting the French Academy's rules, his original ideas and techniques led to completely new painting concepts and approaches for artists.

★

PAINTING EN PLEIN AIR

While still at school in Le Havre, Monet earned money selling caricatures of local people. Then, a landscape painter, Eugène Boudin (1824–98), took him on painting trips, to show him how to paint en plein air. He soon went to Paris to study art, where he met Renoir, Pissarro, Frédéric Bazille (1841–70) and Alfred Sisley (1839–99). Following the Barbizon painters, they all began painting in the countryside.

The Beach at Trouville, Claude Monet, 1870, oil on canvas, The National Gallery, London, UK.

JAPANESE PRINTS

Monet began collecting Japanese woodblock prints in the 1860s. Japanese artists' approach to art was different from Western artists, and Monet particularly admired their simplified, flat-looking and colourful pictures (see the image of the sea on page 70).

EIGHT ART SHOWS

Monet went on painting trips with Renoir, usually around Paris. Annoyed with the Academy's rejections of their work, he and his friends decided to hold their own exhibitions, and between 1874 and 1888, the Impressionists put on eight **independent** shows. At first, critics laughed at Monet's work, but later they liked it.

THE SALON DES REFUSÉS

In 1863, so much art had been rejected from the Paris Salon by the Academy, that Emperor Napoleon arranged for a special exhibition for it all. At the 'Salon des Refusés' (the exhibition of the rejected) Monet first saw one of Manet's paintings, and loved it. After a difficult start, the two artists became friends.

Bathers at La Grenouillère, Claude Monet, 1869, oil on canvas, The National Gallery, London, UK. A scene from one of Monet's painting trips with Renoir. This was a boating and bathing lake with a floating café outside Paris.

THE HOSCHEDÉS

One admirer of Monet's paintings was Ernest Hoschedé, a wealthy businessman. Ernest, his wife Alice and their children became close friends with Monet and his family. Years later, when Monet's wife and Ernest had both died, Monet married Alice.

The Thames Below Westminster, Claude Monet, c.1871, oil on canvas, The National Gallery, London, UK. Monet's misty, atmospheric painting of London when he was staying there during the Franco-Prussian war.

LONDON

Monet struggled to earn a living. In 1870, war broke out in France and he and his new wife Camille and their young son escaped to London. There he painted and met up with Pissarro, and the two men saw paintings by Constable and Turner in The National Gallery.

The Water-Lily Pond, Claude Monet, 1899, oil on canvas, The National Gallery, London, UK. One of 17 views Monet painted of the Japanese bridge he had built over his lily pond.

DREAM GARDEN

In the 1880s, Monet's fortunes began to improve. His paintings sold well and he began creating the garden of his dreams at his home in the village of Giverny. Apart from further painting trips to London and Venice, he spent most of the rest of his life in his garden, painting hundreds of works, including around 250 of his lily pond.

Post-Impressionism

From about 1880, some artists, inspired by the Impressionists, began using bolder colours, distinctive brushwork and often thick paint. They developed their ideas independently, so there was no one style or technique, but they were all later called Post-Impressionists.

HUGE IMPACT

Overall, the Post-Impressionists had a huge impact on several later art movements. Their experiments with colour, line, shape and form freed art from the conventional way of observing and depicting the world. As well as showing what they saw, they also showed some of their feelings and opinions.

DIFFERENT VIEWPOINTS

Some of the most famous Post-Impressionists include Paul Gauguin (1848–1903), Vincent van Gogh (1853–90), Henri de Toulouse-Lautrec (1864–1901) and Henri Rousseau (1844–1910). Paul Cézanne (1839–1906) also became one of the greatest modern artists associated with this diverse group. During his life his art was misunderstood, but he aimed to show the structure of things, so he painted from different viewpoints at once, using small, repetitive brushstrokes. His shapes and blocks of colour later led to the development of **Cubism**.

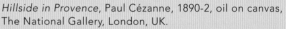

Hillside in Provence, Paul Cézanne, 1890-2, oil on canvas, The National Gallery, London, UK.

Surprised!, Henri Rousseau, 1891, oil on canvas, The National Gallery, London, UK.

THE JUNGLE AND NIGHTLIFE

Rousseau is known for his colourful jungle scenes. His childlike style is sometimes called Primitivism. Toulouse-Lautrec became famous for his prints, posters and paintings of Parisian nightlife. He did not flatter his subjects, and painted curving outlines and vibrant colours.

Art Lesson

Paint a bowl of fruit like Gauguin. Gauguin used colour in entirely new ways. Draw a bowl of fruit, and using flat brushmarks, paint them in bright, sometimes unexpected colours, such as purple for shadows and outlines, orange patches on a banana, pink grapes!

EXPRESSIVE BRUSHSTROKES

Gauguin's brightly coloured, flat-looking, symbolic style is also called Synthetism or Cloisonnism. Van Gogh's dramatic brushstrokes, thick paint, vivid colours and powerful symbolism have made him one of the most famous Post-Impressionists, even though he was almost completely unknown during his lifetime (see pages 70–71).

COLOURED DOTS

The art of Georges Seurat (1859–91) is also called Neo-Impressionism (New Impressionism), **Pointillism** or Divisionism. Fascinated by scientific colour theories, he painted dots of pure colour side-by-side across his canvases – like pixels – believing that this made his pictures appear brighter. For instance, he believed that red and yellow dots together make a brighter orange than if mixed together then painted.

NEW SUBJECTS AND TECHNIQUES

The name **Post-Impressionism** was invented by the English art critic Roger Fry in 1910 after most of the artists concerned had died. Although the Impressionists painted the light and fleeting moments, the Post-Impressionists were more concerned with colour and form. They believed that their colourful creations were more relevant to modern life than detailed, lifelike works of art.

Bathers at Asnières, Georges Seurat, 1884, oil on canvas, The National Gallery, London, UK. Seurat is developing his idea about dots here in the boy's red hat.

Van Gogh

Today Vincent van Gogh (1853–90) is one of the most famous painters in the world, but throughout his life, he was poor and unrecognized.

DIFFERENT JOBS

Born in Holland, Van Gogh had many jobs before he became a painter, including working in a bookshop, an art gallery, as a teacher and a preacher. He decided to be an artist aged 27, and by the time he died just 10 years later, he had produced over 2,000 works.

Sunflowers, Vincent van Gogh, 1888, oil on canvas, The National Gallery, London, UK. Van Gogh painted seven different versions of this painting.

INFLUENCES

Fascinated by a wide variety of art, at first Van Gogh followed Millet's example and painted peasants. In the early 1880s, he studied paintings by Rembrandt, Hals and Rubens. Then, living in Belgium in 1885, he discovered Japanese prints. He loved their simple designs and flat, bright colours. In 1886, he moved to Paris. There he discovered how Delacroix, the Impressionists and some of the Post-Impressionists used colour. Since 1868, Japanese prints had become available, and Van Gogh began collecting them and using some of their ideas in his paintings.

The Great Wave at Kanagawa, Katsushika Hokusai, c.1831–3, polychrome ink and colour on paper, The Metropolitan Museum of Art, New York, USA. A Japanese print of the Edo period, featuring all the elements that Van Gogh loved: bold, flat colour, simple shapes and fluid lines.

BOLD COLOURS

While living in Paris with his art dealer brother Theo, Van Gogh mixed with the Impressionists and other artists including Émile Bernard (1868–1941) and Toulouse-Lautrec. His palette changed from the dark colours of his early paintings to bright complementary colours, and his brushwork became thicker and more expressive.

MENTAL INSTITUTION

Van Gogh had been suffering with mental problems and when he and Paul Gauguin had a big argument, he cut off part of his earlobe and eventually admitted himself to a mental hospital. There, he continued to paint, applying dashes and swirls of thick (impasto) paint in intense colours.

A Wheatfield with Cypresses, Vincent van Gogh, 1889, oil on canvas, The National Gallery, London, UK. This was painted after his time in the asylum.

AUVERS-SUR-OISE

Despite his stay in the asylum, Van Gogh's health never really improved. In May 1890, he moved to a village just outside Paris, to be near his new doctor, and brother Theo. For two months, he produced roughly a painting a day, then in July, he shot himself. He died two days later.

Chair, Vincent van Gogh, 1888, oil on canvas, The National Gallery, London, UK. Yellow symbolized happiness for Van Gogh.

LEGACY

Van Gogh's subjects included portraits, self-portraits, ordinary people at daily tasks, interior scenes, landscapes, still lifes and flowers. His unique style influenced several other movements, especially **Fauvism** and **Expressionism**.

Symbolism and Art Nouveau

At the end of the 19th century, while many artists represented real life, others created mysterious pictures from their imaginations, the ancient past or stories and legends. They became known as **Symbolists**.

FEELINGS AND IMPRESSIONS

Symbolists painted a wide variety of subjects, including heroes, women, animals, flowers and landscapes, but symbolized things like love, death, sorrow or dreams. Unlike the direct symbols in Renaissance paintings, such as in Jan van Eyck's *Arnolfini Portrait* (see page 26), Symbolists merely hinted at or made vague suggestions about feelings or impressions.

Lake Keitele, Akseli Gallen-Kallela, 1905, oil on canvas, The National Gallery, London, UK.

HIDDEN MEANINGS

Symbolism had featured in art for centuries, and can be seen in paintings by Gauguin, but by about 1880, artists including Gustave Moreau (1826–98), Odilon Redon (1840–1916) and Pierre Puvis de Chavannes (1824–98) produced pictures that deliberately show one thing but suggest other meanings.

Saint George and the Dragon, Gustave Moreau, 1889–90, oil on canvas, The National Gallery, London, UK.

DIFFERENT COUNTRIES, DIFFERENT STYLES

Symbolism began in France where the Impressionists and Post-Impressionists were working, although other Symbolist painters emerged in Russia, Belgium and Austria, including Fernand Khnopff (1858–1921), Gustav Klimt (1862–1918), Jan Toorop (1858–1928), Edvard Munch (1863–1944) and Akseli Gallen-Kallela (1865–1931). The artists did not call themselves Symbolists, or see themselves as part of one movement. All their styles are different, they were just grouped together under the name later.

NEW ART

Another movement of the same time, closely linked to Symbolism, was Art Nouveau. It appeared in painting, sculpture, jewellery, metalwork, glass, ceramics, textiles, graphic design, furniture and architecture, and it developed differently in many places around the world. Blending ideas from Western and Eastern art, it was given different names in different countries, including Jugendstil, Modern Style, Stile Liberty, Tiffany Style and Glasgow Style.

Although every artist and designer interpreted the ideas individually, there were certain common characteristics, including curving, flowing lines, **asymmetrical** compositions, glowing colours, sinuous shapes and a focus on the natural world.

LES NABIS

As the three art movements of Post-Impressionism, Symbolism and Art Nouveau happened simultaneously, there are several overlaps. A group of Post-Impressionists who called themselves '**Les Nabis**', which means The Prophets in Hebrew and Arabic, shared many aims and ideas with both Art Nouveau and Symbolism. Its main members were Pierre Bonnard (1867–1947) who painted dreamlike pictures from memory, Édouard Vuillard (1868–1940) who used flat, decorative colours, Ker-Xavier Roussel (1867–1944), Félix Vallotton (1865–1925) and Maurice Denis (1870–1943).

Cubism, Futurism

AND THE BIRTH OF ABSTRACT ART

In the autumn of 1906, Pablo Picasso (1881–1973) went to an exhibition in Paris of Cézanne's work. Cézanne had spent most of his career trying to show structure, so his images often contained angular lines. They had an immense impact on Picasso.

★

BROKEN FRAGMENTS

Picasso and his friend Georges Braque (1882–1963) took Cézanne's ideas even further. Rather than follow traditional rules of painting perspective to show three dimensions on flat canvases, they painted objects from several angles at once. Using few colours, their depictions looked like broken fragments, and when a critic described one of Braque's paintings as looking like 'little cubes', the name Cubism stuck. From 1908 to 1912, their style became known as 'Analytical Cubism'. After 1912, they began using more colours and often **collage** as well, and the phase became known as 'Synthetic Cubism'.

Houses at L'Estaque, Georges Braque, 1908, oil on canvas, Lille Métropole Museum of Modern, Contemporary and Outsider Art (LaM), Villeneuve d'Ascq, France. This painting was described by an art critic as looking like 'little cubes'.

Make your own Cubist collage! Picasso and Braque often stuck bits of newspaper, wallpaper and other objects on their paintings. Draw a group of objects and paint or colour in some areas. Then stick down things that show what your objects are – perhaps a piece of cloth or magazine, a ticket or a button – be imaginative!

Unique Forms of Continuity in Space, Umberto Boccioni, 1913, bronze, Tate, London, UK.

ART AND MUSIC

Wassily Kandinsky (1866–1944) began a series of paintings in 1910 of just colours and shapes, not representing anything from the real world. It was a complete break with the past. Kandinsky had been painting distorted images of the real world, but he soon began abandoning all references to recognizable things. He and some other abstract artists believed that just like music, art did not have to imitate 'real' things.

Influenced by several recent art movements, including Post-Impressionism and Cubism, abstract art developed individually with different artists. Kandinsky, for instance, aimed to express feelings through shapes and colours, just as music does with sounds. He thought that colours and shapes could express various things through tone, composition and harmony just as music does.

DESTROY IT!

Another new art movement was launched in 1909 in Italy, and the artists chose a name for it: **Futurism**. Futurists were excited about the modern world, particularly machines, cars, planes and cities. They wanted to forget the history of Italian art – from the ancient Romans to the Renaissance and the Baroque, and even to destroy their museums! Artists included Carlo Carrà (1881–1966), Umberto Boccioni (1882–1916), Gino Severini (1883–1966) and Giacomo Balla (1871–1958). They used colours, lines and shapes in almost abstract ways to convey excitement, speed and energy.

Picasso

One of the greatest artists of the 20th century, Pablo Picasso showed great talent from an early age. When he was 19, he left his native Spain and moved to Paris where he met many famous artists.

BLUE AND ROSE PERIODS

In 1901, his close friend Carlos Casagemas committed suicide. Picasso was grief-stricken. For the next three years he painted sad-looking, elongated figures, mainly in shades of blue. From 1904, his pictures became a bit happier and painted in shades of pink. These two phases were later labelled his Blue and Rose periods.

WEALTHY COLLECTORS

In 1905, the wealthy American art collectors Leo and Gertrude Stein began to collect Picasso's work and helped to make him famous. In 1907, inspired by Cézanne and by Spanish and African sculpture, Picasso painted *Les Demoiselles d'Avignon*, which is often described as the first truly modern painting. It features many things, such as aspects inspired by African masks, some things shown from different viewpoints at once, and some parts not even finished. All this affected the future of painting, and led directly to Picasso's invention of Cubism (see pages 74–75).

Les Demoiselles d'Avignon, Pablo Picasso, 1907, oil on canvas, Museum of Modern Art, New York, USA.

Guernica, Pablo Picasso, 1937, oil on canvas, Museo Reina Sofia, Madrid, Spain. A huge and powerful statement showing the suffering and tragedies of war.

GUERNICA

In 1937, there was a civil war in Spain. Appalled by the bombing of the Spanish town of Guernica, Picasso produced a huge painting, called *Guernica*. Showing the suffering caused by war, and especially by civil war, the enormous black-and-white painting helped to bring the horrors and devastation of the Spanish Civil War to the world's attention.

✪ Did you know?

When Picasso first lived in Paris, he and his friend were so poor that they only had one bed between them and had to take it in turns to sleep! While one painted, the other slept in the bed.

STATUES AND DREAMS

From around 1921, Picasso began borrowing ideas from Renaissance artists, making his painted figures look solid like statues. By 1924, he became interested in another new movement called **Surrealism**, which explored dreams and unconscious thoughts.

INSPIRING INFLUENCES

Constantly exploring and experimenting, Picasso never worked in one style for long, but invented and participated in many different art movements. Inspired by many things, including his surroundings, his girlfriends and wives, Cézanne, Matisse, the ballet and Spanish and African art, Picasso was always original. His art explored humans and their situations.

THOUSANDS OF WORKS

Over his career, Picasso produced oil paintings, sculpture, drawings, stage designs, costumes, tapestries, rugs, ceramics, etchings and collage. He never stopped working and produced a vast number of artworks, including 1,885 paintings, 1,228 sculptures, 2,880 ceramics, roughly 12,000 drawings and thousands of prints.

Wild and expressive

THE EARLY 20TH CENTURY

In 1903, as a reaction to the official Salon that was held each spring, another annual exhibition was organized in Paris that was more open-minded about art.

Portrait of Greta Moll, Henri Matisse, 1908, oil on canvas, The National Gallery, London, UK.

HENRI MATISSE

Nicknamed the 'King of Colour', Matisse was considered the leader of the Fauves. Influenced by the Impressionists, Cézanne, Seurat, Gauguin and Van Gogh, he is known for his bold use of bright colours. He said he wanted to create art that everyone could enjoy, 'like a good armchair'.

THE SALON D'AUTOMNE

The exhibition became called the Salon d'Automne (autumn exhibition). In 1905, Henri Matisse (1869–1954), Maurice de Vlaminck (1876–1958), André Derain (1880–1954), Raoul Dufy (1877–1953) and Braque exhibited there. Using free brushstrokes and bright, exaggerated colours, they tried to express joyful feelings and create a new art. A critic at the exhibition declared the paintings were like wild beasts ('les fauves' in French), and the movement came to be called Fauvism.

NEW EMOTIONS

In the early 1900s, in various cities across Germany, some artists felt uncomfortable about things they saw in their society, such as greed and a lack of spirituality. Inspired by Van Gogh, Munch, James Ensor (1860–1949) and Marc Chagall (1887–1985) they began expressing their feelings and concerns in paint. Art was changing. Instead of being what artists saw, it was now what artists felt. The German artists' work was often distorted, disturbing and vividly coloured. The movement was called **Expressionism**.

Paint your feelings like the Expressionists! Use oil pastels and a big sheet of paper. Filling the paper, draw something you feel strongly about. If you feel cross, make jagged marks, if you feel happy, create soft marks. Exaggerate your colours!

The Scream, Edvard Munch, 1893, tempera and crayon on cardboard, National Gallery, Oslo, Norway. Based on a dream, Munch produced four versions of this, in paint and pastel.

THE BRIDGE

There were several Expressionist groups. Forming in 1905, one group called 'Die Brücke' (The Bridge) aimed to bridge the gap between art of the past and art of the future. It included Ernst Ludwig Kirchner (1880–1938), Emil Nolde (1867–1956) and Karl Schmidt-Rottluff (1884–1976). Many of their paintings were troubling, out of proportion and strongly coloured.

The Fate of the Animals, Franz Marc, 1913, oil on canvas, Kunstmuseum, Basel, Switzerland.

BLAUE REITER

Another Expressionist group formed in 1911. Called 'Der Blaue Reiter' (The Blue Rider), it was formed by Kandinsky, who was Russian but living in Germany at that time, and Franz Marc (1880–1916). Marc loved painting horses and other animals, and Kandinsky believed that blue was a calming, spiritual colour.

79

Art of the mind

DADAISM AND SURREALISM

In 1916, some artists gathered in Zurich, Switzerland, which was neutral (did not take sides) during World War I. Appalled by the horrors of the war the artists began creating strange and shocking art in protest. They said it was anti-art and they deliberately picked a random name for it from a dictionary. '**Dada**' means hobby horse in French and 'yes yes' in Russian! Dada ideas soon spread across Europe and America.

POKING FUN

Dada deliberately poked fun at artistic traditions. Marcel Duchamp drew a moustache on a print of *Mona Lisa* (see page 31). Other Dadaists made messy collages or rubbings, as they said while humans were killing each other in the war, what was the point of making skilful, beautiful art?

✪ Did you know?

One of the most famous Dada works was exhibited by Marcel Duchamp in 1917. It was a urinal that he called *Fountain*, signed 'R. Mutt' and displayed upside-down! Viewers were horrified, but Duchamp was challenging the idea that all art had to be made by a skilled, known artist. For him, ideas behind art were far more important than creative skills. This type of art using existing objects is called **readymade**.

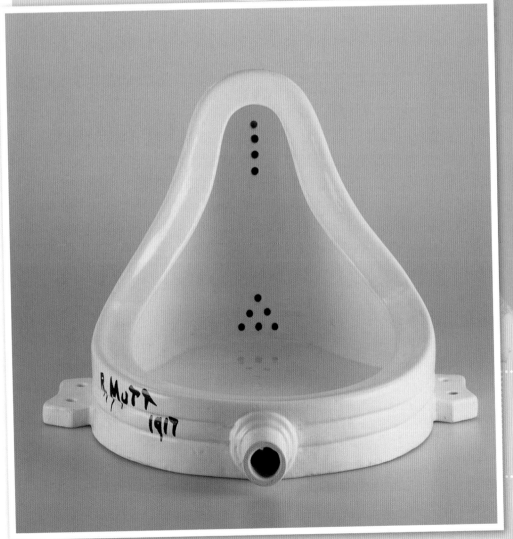

Fountain, Marcel Duchamp, 1917 (replica 1964), porcelain, Tate Modern, London, UK.

Make a Surrealist picture. Use paint, pens and pictures cut out from magazines. Draw a weird, dreamlike scene. Put odd things in unexpected places, either drawn or using magazine pictures glued down. Draw, colour or paint to fill the picture.

THE UNCONSCIOUS MIND

In 1924, six years after the end of World War I, Surrealism developed, partly from Dada ideas, and partly to explore the findings of Sigmund Freud (1856–1939), a doctor who had discovered that dreams can help us understand our unconscious minds. He believed that we are unaware of many important thoughts and feelings that are buried in our minds. Surrealists tried to uncover all these things.

Persistence of Memory, Salvador Dalí, 1931, oil on canvas, Museum of Modern Art, New York, USA. One of Dalí's dreamlike paintings.

Time Transfixed, René Magritte, 1938, oil on canvas, The Art Institute of Chicago, Michigan, USA. Why is a train coming out of a fireplace? Why does only one candlestick have a reflection?

MORE THAN REAL

Surrealism means 'above realism' or 'more than real', and Surrealists had two main ways of working. Some produced realistic looking paintings that are like weird dreams or nightmares. Others drew or painted, purposely not thinking, so their images came from their unconscious minds. This is called '**automatism**', and some Surrealist writers also did this with words. The most famous Surrealists included Salvador Dalí (1904–89), who said he made "hand painted dream photographs", René Magritte (1893–1967), who painted odd **juxtapositions**, such as a man with an apple for a head, Joan Miró (1893–1983), who practised automatism, Max Ernst (1891–1976), Yves Tanguy (1900–55) and Man Ray (1890–1976).

Shapes and colours

SUPREMATISM, CONSTRUCTIVISM, DE STIJL

When Dada was at its peak, some other art movements emerged elsewhere in Europe. World War I lasted from 1914 to 1918, and in 1917, there were two revolutions in Russia.

★

Suprematist Composition (with Black Trapezium and Red Square), Kazimir Malevich, 1915, oil on canvas, Stedelijk Museum, Amsterdam, The Netherlands.

SUPREMATISM

Suprematism began in Russia in 1915, started by Kazimir Malevich (1878–1935) when he painted a large black square on a white background. He saw this as the ultimate balance of positive and negative, as pure emotion because there was nothing from the world we recognize. Inspired partly by Cubism and Futurism, and partly by his spiritual beliefs, Malevich continued to paint many arrangements of coloured geometric shapes. He believed that this pure abstraction had great spiritual power and would give viewers 'the supremacy of pure feeling' (perfect, clear thoughts). He felt Suprematism suited the newly organized Russia, but although they liked it initially, the authorities soon stopped approving of Suprematism.

82

INSPIRING FUTURE DESIGN

Constructivists often created objects in three dimensions as they aimed to help create a new Russian society with perfectly balanced art, buildings and furniture. At first, **Constructivism** was seen by many as meeting the goals of the Revolution, but the new government soon began favouring realistic art. Both Suprematism and Constructivism had a powerful influence on abstract art and design styles of the 20th century.

Composition with Red, Blue and Yellow, Piet Mondrian, 1930, oil on canvas, Kunsthaus, Zurich, Switzerland.

DE STIJL

In the Netherlands in 1917, Piet Mondrian (1872–1944) and Theo van Doesberg (1883–1931) founded the journal '**De Stijl**' (The Style). It attracted a group of artists, designers and architects. Trying to create the purest forms possible, they simplified all the elements of their paintings and buildings. Mondrian had the most original ideas. He aimed to develop a new 'visual language' that everybody could appreciate, expressing the harmony, balance, peace and rhythms of the universe with only primary colours and black grid lines on white or grey grounds. He called this spiritual theory Neoplasticism and it influenced his work until his death in 1944.

CONSTRUCTIVISM

Borrowing ideas from Suprematism as well as Cubism and Futurism, Constructivism developed in about 1917. Focusing on geometric shapes and forms, like Malevich, the Constructivists also abandoned traditional artistic styles. Unlike Suprematism though, Constructivism was not about spiritual ideas. It was simply intended to be understood by everyone and for all art – painting, design and architecture – to have one style. The main Constructivists were Vladimir Tatlin (1885–1953), Alexander Rodchenko (1891–1956), El Lissitzky (1890–1941) and Naum Gabo (1890–1977).

The new century

IN THE AMERICAS

In the late 19th and early 20th centuries in America, art movements and ideas developed independently from European movements. Even American Realism differed from French Realism.

AMERICAN REALISM

Thomas Eakins (1844–1916) was an American Realist who from the early 1870s painted detailed pictures of real life. He produced hundreds of portraits, usually of friends, members of his family or people in the arts, sciences, medicine and clergy.

ASHCAN SCHOOL

Developing from American Realism, several artists began painting daily life in poor neighbourhoods of New York and some other cities. They became known as the Ashcan School because of the harsh realities they painted. Famous Ashcan artists are Robert Henri (1865–1929), John Sloan (1871–1951), Everett Shinn (1876–1953) and George Bellows (1882–1925). Edward Hopper (1882–1967) is often linked with them, but he said his work did not show rough elements of life, simply parts of America and American life that were not always seen.

✪ Did you know?

In October 1929, the Wall Street stock market crashed. This huge financial disaster affected the whole world and it became known as the Great Depression. Millions of people lost their jobs and their money.

O'KEEFFE AND STIEGLITZ

America was more open-minded towards female artists than Europe, and Georgia O'Keeffe (1887–1986) found success painting pictures that sometimes bordered on abstraction. Her work is often called Precisionist, which was an American style influenced by photography and Cubism. O'Keeffe's career took off after some of her abstract drawings were shown to an influential photographer and gallery owner, Alfred Stieglitz (1864–1946). He put on an exhibition for her in 1917, and in 1924 they were married!

American Gothic, Grant Wood, 1930, oil on canvas, The Art Institute of Chicago, Michigan, USA. The detailed, rigid figures and house make this one of America's most famous paintings.

Oriental Poppies, Georgia O'Keeffe, 1928, oil on canvas, Frederick R. Weisman Art Museum, Minneapolis, USA. O'Keeffe said she painted oversized flowers to surprise people.

REGIONALISM

To restore confidence in America, some artists began painting the quiet, hard-working lives of people in small towns and the country. The movement was called Regionalism and the main artists included Grant Wood (1892–1942) and Thomas Hart Benton (1889–1975).

MEXICAN MURALISTS

From 1910 to 1920, a civil war and a Revolution were fought in Mexico. At the end of the Revolution the government commissioned artists to create art to educate ordinary people about Mexican history. The Mexican Muralists, who included Diego Rivera (1886–1957), José Clemente Orozco (1883–1949) and David Alfaro Siqueiros (1896–1974), produced large, colourful wall paintings, mixing images from Mexico's troubled past, folk art and the art of the ancient Mexicans – the Mayans and Aztecs. The artists hoped their paintings would help to bring ordinary Mexicans together after the troubles.

Colour and feeling

ABSTRACT EXPRESSIONISM

Even after World War II, peace was fragile and life was difficult for many. Several artists tried to express their deep feelings about all that had happened and what was happening as life started again after the fighting.

ACTION MEN

In 1947, Jackson Pollock (1912–56) began experimenting with a radically different way of painting. Laying his canvases on the floor rather than on an easel, he dripped, poured and spattered paint all over it. For him, his unconscious process of painting was as important as the work itself. For his style of painting, *Time* magazine nicknamed him 'Jack the Dripper'! Willem De Kooning (1904–97) was the only Abstract Expressionist to paint people as well as abstract works. His vibrant images are packed with energy and emotion.

INTERNATIONAL IMPACT

Abstract Expressionism was the first art movement to begin in the USA that had an international impact. As many Surrealists had fled to America from Europe during the war, they influenced the new movement. Yet Abstract Expressionism did not follow Surrealist dream paintings. Instead, most Abstract Expressionists built on the ideas of **automatism**, so their paintings emerged from their innermost thoughts and feelings.

Number 1, 1950 (Lavender Mist), Jackson Pollock, 1950, oil, enamel and aluminum on canvas, National Gallery of Art, Washington DC, USA.

LEADING THE ART WORLD

Until World War II, Western art had been dominated by European artists, particularly those in Paris. New movements and influences had sometimes emerged from elsewhere, but after the war, for the first time, New York became the centre of world art.

Red, Orange, Orange on Red, Mark Rothko, 1962, oil on canvas, St Louis Art Museum, Missouri, USA.

COLOUR PATCHES

Armenian-born Arshile Gorky (1904–48) began his artistic career as a Surrealist, and ended it as an Abstract Expressionist. He moved to America in 1920 when he was 16, and experimented with several styles before creating spontaneous, patchy and colourful abstract paintings that suggest many things at once.

TWO STYLES

Although all Abstract Expressionist paintings were individual, two distinct styles emerged. One was the **Action Painting** of artists like Gorky, Pollock and De Kooning, and the other was the **Colour Field** process explored by artists including Mark Rothko (1903–70), Barnett Newman (1905–70) and Clyfford Still (1904–80). Colour Field paintings usually contain several large blocks of intense colour, in no particular shapes. Viewers are expected to consider the feelings the paintings inspire as they look at them. Frank Stella (born 1936) helped to inspire Colour Field. Exploring energy and size, he painted complicated arrangements of lines and shapes in smooth colours. Constantly experimenting, he also produced sculpture and prints, and helped to inspire **Minimalism** and **Post-Painterly Abstraction**.

POW! WHAAM!

POP AND OP ART

In 1956 in London, some artists put on an exhibition they called 'This is Tomorrow'. Their art used images from advertising, newspapers, pop music and magazines.

★

FUN ART

This new art became called **Pop art**. It was made for modern people who were familiar with advertising, packaging, TV, films, celebrities and magazines, but not necessarily with traditional art in museums. It was meant to be fun. Soon after this, in America, other painters and sculptors produced art based on similar ideas. All the artists were trying to get away from recent art movements, particularly Abstract Expressionism, which they thought was self-centred and focused on the idea of the brushmark and the identity of the artist. They wanted to produce art that everyone could feel part of but that also challenged ideas about making and 'marks'.

Campbell's Tomato Soup Can, Andy Warhol, 1962, synthetic polymer paint on canvas, Museum of Modern Art, New York, USA.

CONSUMERISM

After World War II, more mass-produced goods were available, and more people were buying them. This is called consumerism, and artists like Andy Warhol (1928–87) said that like pop music, art should reflect consumerism, and depict things that people could relate to, such as food packaging.

PLAYING TRICKS

Another art movement developed simultaneously. The name Pop art came from 'popular', but Op art came from 'optical illusions'. Op artists used lines, colours and patterns on flat canvases to create optical illusions when we look at them. Some seem to move, roll or vibrate! Leading Op artists are Victor Vasarely (1906–97), Bridget Riley (born 1931), Richard Anuszkiewicz (born 1930) and Jesus Rafael Soto (1923–2005).

⭐ Did you know?

Richard Hamilton (1922–2011) made this list of what he thought Pop art should be: "popular, transient, expendable, low-cost, mass-produced, young, witty, sexy, gimmicky, glamorous and big business!"

ANDY WARHOL

One of the most famous Pop artists, Warhol produced images of things like soup cans, celebrities and news stories. In his large workshop which he called 'The Factory', assistants helped him as in Renaissance workshops, but many complained that if assistants made it, it was not art. Warhol said anything is art if we say it is, no matter who makes it. His ideas radically changed the path of art.

Supermarket Shopper, Duane Hanson, 1970, polyester resin and fibreglass, polychromed in oil, mixed media with accessories, Neue Galerie, Sammlung Ludwig, Aachen, Germany.

Whaam!, Roy Lichtenstein, 1963, acrylic and oil paint on canvas, Tate, London, UK. Lichtenstein developed the idea for this attention-grabbing painting from a comic.

DIFFERENT IDEAS

Leading Pop artists include Richard Hamilton, Peter Blake (born 1932), David Hockney (born 1937), Andy Warhol, Jasper Johns (born 1930), Roy Lichtenstein (1923–97), Claes Oldenburg (born 1929), Duane Hanson (1925–96) and Wayne Thiebaud (born 1920). All their ideas were different. For instance, Lichtenstein painted cartoons with large dots like those used in printing. Oldenburg created 'soft sculptures', such as hamburgers or toothbrushes made with soft materials. Thiebaud produced colourful paintings of ordinary objects such as cakes and lipsticks.

Post-Modernism

AND CONTEMPORARY ART

Although most of this book is about paintings, since the 1980s, artists have used a broader range of materials, from computers, lights and videos, to skulls, food and building materials.

NEW MEDIA

Nam June Paik (1932–2006) is considered the founder of video art, and Bill Viola (born 1951) uses video to explore spirituality and life experiences. Jake Tilson (born 1958) is one of many artists to use the Internet as new **media** for his art. Cindy Sherman (born 1954) has explored stereotypes through photographs, and Gerhard Richter (born 1932) has painted over photographs to create images.

ART OF IDEAS

Contemporary art is often more about ideas than traditional methods of making art. Picasso and Duchamp started this when they used different picture surfaces. When Warhol said that anything can be art, he also changed attitudes.

In the 1950s, some artists such as Joseph Beuys (1921–86) and Allan Kaprow (1927–2006) gave performances, which came to be called Performance art. Performance art and another movement, Conceptualism, consider how our actions shape the world around us. As part of Conceptualism and Minimalism, in the 1960s, Dan Flavin (1933–96) created installations using neon lights, and in the 1970s, Carl Andre (born 1935) caused a scandal by exhibiting bricks and blocks of metal or wood.

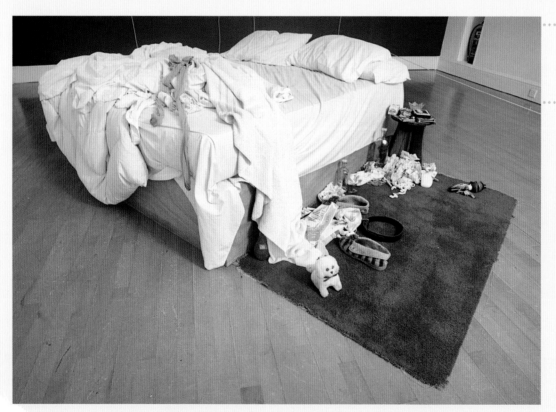

My Bed, Tracey Emin, 1998, mattress, linens, pillows, objects, Private Collection.

YBAs

Damien Hirst (born 1965) and Tracey Emin (born 1963) are grouped with the YBAs (Young British Artists) who first exhibited together in London in 1988. Using unexpected materials, their art was deliberately shocking.

PAINTING

But painting is not dead! Many artists continue to paint, from the graffiti style of Keith Haring (1958–90) to the Hyperrealism of Chuck Close (born 1940). From David Hockney's iPad pictures to the spin paintings of Damien Hirst, and from the witty, lively paintings of Paula Rego (born 1935) to the huge figure paintings of Jenny Saville (born 1970). Francis Bacon (1909–92), made expressive, emotional paintings and Lucien Freud (1922–2011) painted thick, impasto portraits and figures.

EARTH OR LAND ART

Some artists use the landscape to make art. After carving earthworks in the land or creating structures using natural materials, many Land artists take photographs of their work before it decays or disappears. The most famous **Land art** is *Spiral Jetty* by Robert Smithson (1938–73), a giant spiral in the Great Salt Lake in America, made of mud, salt crystals, rocks and water. Other Land artists include Richard Long (born 1945) and Andy Goldsworthy (born 1956).

Art Lesson

As you can see, art changes constantly! Artists will always make art and it will always make people think. Picasso probably summed it up when he said: 'Art is a lie that makes us realize truth'.

Spiral Jetty, Robert Smithson, 1970, mud, precipitated salt crystals, rocks, water, Great Salt Lake, Utah, USA. Depending on the water levels around it, this can sometimes be seen and is sometimes submerged.

CREATE YOUR OWN
Art Gallery

★

THE NATIONAL GALLERY

Situated in Trafalgar Square, London, The National Gallery was founded in 1824 and houses more than 2,300 works of art. The earliest piece is from the 13th century and the latest is from 1912. All the images in your app are housed in The National Gallery.

Almost all of the artworks you've seen in this book are housed in a public art gallery, so that everyone can enjoy looking at them. Galleries take good care of the artwork so that it doesn't deteriorate or get damaged, and this is why we are able to look at paintings that are hundreds of years old. Galleries are divided into rooms, and curators decide which pieces to group together in a room. Use your app to curate the rooms in your art gallery!

The main National Gallery building opened in 1838. Trafalgar Square was chosen because it could be reached easily by both rich people from west London and the poor from the east.

THEME YOUR GALLERY'S ROOMS

Think about how you want to hang the works in your gallery before you start. Will you put them in chronological order, like many large galleries do, or maybe you'll group them by colour? Look at the themes of the paintings – are some religious, or do some show people or animals? Perhaps you'll just want to hang your favourites together! Have fun expressing yourself and your ideas, then invite others to come and view your exhibition.

The rooms in the National Gallery are grouped chronologically. Room 35 (above right) shows 18th-century British paintings. Room 60 (left) displays Italian paintings from 1490 to 1510 by artists including Raphael. Room 29 (right) contains Flemish paintings from the early 17th century by Peter Paul Rubens and Anthony van Dyck.

ACTIVATE YOUR APP

Hold your device up to these pages!

⭐ Download your free app to create your own virtual gallery. Hang paintings from The National Gallery on the walls of your gallery, and upload your own pictures to place next to them. Decide how you're going to theme each room in the gallery, but remember there's no right or wrong – it's up to you!

⭐ Then test your art knowledge by playing the games included with the app. Can you… piece together the jigsaw of a famous painting? Spot the differences between two paintings? Pick the odd one out from a group of paintings? Give it a go!

Glossary

Abstract Expressionism – expressive, usually abstract painting from the 1940s, 50s and 60s

Action painting – a method of painting when artists drip, splatter or throw paint at canvases

Art movement – a type or style of art that happens at a similar time. Some are planned by artists, others are not and are defined afterwards

Asymmetrical – not the same on each side

Atmosphere – the air in a locality

Automatism – a spontaneous technique of painting and writing when artists or authors do not think consciously

Baroque – starting in Rome in the 17th century, a type of art that made Catholic beliefs exciting and dramatic

Blaue Reiter, Der (The Blue Rider) – an early Expressionist group that aimed to create spiritual feelings through painting

Brücke, Die – part of Expressionism, painting featuring intense colours, a flat style and heavy outlines

Ceramics – objects made from clay and hardened with heat

Chiaroscuro – Italian for 'light-dark', strong tonal contrasts created to make pictures more dramatic

Classical – a general term to describe the lifelike art of the ancient Greeks and Romans

Collage – mixtures of materials either cut or torn and stuck on a work of art

Colour Field – a type of Abstract Expressionism from the 1960s with densely coloured canvases

Colour wheel – a circle divided into different coloured sections that shows relationships between colours

Commission – for artists, orders or instructions for works of art to be made

Complementary colours – opposite colours on a colour wheel: blue-orange, yellow-purple, red-green

Constructivism – a Russian abstract art and design movement, using geometric forms for post-Revolutionary Russia

Cubism – a movement where artists aimed to show the 3D world on 2D surfaces, painting from several viewpoints at once

Dada – an anti-art movement created in protest about World War I

Etching – a printing technique used by many artists where a piece of metal is engraved with lines

Expressionism – art that expresses feelings, so colours and shapes can be exaggerated or distorted

Fauvism – from 1905, a loose group of artists who painted in pure colours to express feelings such as joy

Fête galante – a scene of well-to-do people having fun in the countryside

Flemish – either from Flanders or in the style of things from Flanders (now part of Belgium, France and the Netherlands)

Fresco – paint applied to freshly plastered walls

Futurism – an Italian art movement that celebrated speed, technology, machines and city life

Gothic – medieval art and architecture that expressed Christian beliefs

Impasto – thick layers of paint

Impressionism – a late 19th century art movement that focused on capturing brief moments in time with quick brushmarks and bright colours

Impressionists – artists who belonged to the Impressionist movement

Independent – self-sufficient

Installations – mixed-media constructions usually designed for a certain place and for a short time

Juxtaposition – something placed next to something else

Land art – art connected to the land or environment, using natural materials, often temporary or affected by environmental changes

Linear perspective – uses lines and a vanishing point to make objects further away look smaller

Low relief – material that has been sculpted to look as if it is slightly raised up from the background surface

Media – materials used by artists, the plural of medium

Minimalism – an international art movement since the mid-1960s that uses few elements with no symbolism or emotion

Mosaics – pictures or patterns made from tiny pieces of coloured glass or stone set in plaster

Myths – stories or legends from ancient or Classical times

Nabis, Les – a group of artists who exhibited together at the end of the 19th century, inspired by Gauguin

Neoclassicism (New Classicism) – art of the early 19th century that followed ancient Greek and Roman art styles

Oil paints – paints made by mixing pigment with oil

Palette – both the board that artists mix their paints on, and the range of colours used by individual artists

Palette knife – a blunt tool that looks like a knife, used to mix and apply paint

Patrons – people who buy or commission art

Perspective – ways of showing depth and distance on 2D surfaces

Pointillism – tiny dots of pure, unmixed colour building up a picture

Pop art – a 1950s and 60s art movement that used images from popular culture

Portrait – a likeness, picture or sculpture of a real person

Post-Impressionism – a variety of art styles created straight after Impressionism using bright colours

Post-Painterly Abstraction – a 1960s art movement that developed from Abstract Expressionism using colours in random ways

Primary colours – red, yellow, blue

Print – different methods of making images or words by some form of pressure and ink or paint

Readymade – the name given by Duchamp to certain objects used or exhibited by artists but not made by them

Realism – either lifelike, or a 19th century art movement that showed ordinary, poor people or landscapes with no embellishments

Renaissance, the – an art and cultural movement of the 14th–16th centuries that mixed Classical thinking, science and art with new ideas

Revolution – rebellion, overthrowing of rulers

Rococo – an 18th century decorative and playful art and design style

Romanticism – a late 18th century dramatic and emotional art movement that celebrated nature

Salon, the – a yearly Parisian art exhibition where judges often favoured Classical subjects and traditional styles

Secondary colours – green, purple, orange

Sfumato – Italian for smoky, a soft style of creating shadows in paint, created chiefly by Leonardo da Vinci

Stijl, De – a movement started by Mondrian in 1917, focusing on geometric abstract paintings and designs

Still life – objects that do not move, arrangements for paintings or sculptures

Suprematism – developed by Malevich in 1915, an art movement using only geometric shapes

Surrealism – art that explores our unconscious thoughts and feelings

Symbolism – the use of symbols to represent ideas, and a 19th century art and literary movement that showed ideas, thoughts and dreams rather than reality

Symbolists – members of the Symbolism movement

Tempera – used since ancient times, paint made from mixing dry pigment with egg yolk. It lost popularity when oil paints were made

Tertiary colours – colour made when a primary and secondary colour, or three primary colours are mixed

Three-dimensions – or **3D**, things that are not flat

Vanitas – painting, usually a still life, that reminds us we are alive only for a short time, so we should not be too concerned with worldly goods, possessions and superficial things